THE SUPREME JUDICIARY

October Term 2022

ERWIN CHEMERINSKY

AMERICAN BAR ASSOCIATION
Judicial Division

Cover design by Amanda Fry/ABA Design
Interior design by Betsy Kulak/ABA Design

Printed in the United States of America.

27 26 25 24 23   5 4 3 2 1

ISBN 978-1-63905-402-2
e-ISBN 978-1-63905-403-9

For my grandchildren,
Andrew, Sarah, and Amy

Contents

Preface vii

1 Introduction: October Term 2022 1
2 Affirmative Action 13
3 Civil Rights Statutes 25
4 Criminal Law and Procedure 31
5 Dormant Commerce Clause 45
6 Election Law 53
7 Environmental Law 63
8 Executive Power and State Challenges to It 69
9 Freedom of Speech 77
10 Immigration Law 89
11 Indian Law 101
12 Intellectual Property 109
13 Labor Law 119
14 Personal Jurisdiction 125
15 Conclusion: Looking Ahead 133

Index 139

Preface

For the third year in a row, I feel fortunate to have the opportunity to write this book for the American Bar Association summarizing the Supreme Court's term. October 2022 was, by any measure, another momentous term in the Supreme Court.

These books are a result of a suggestion from Bob Edmunds and Herbert Dixon that I provide a written description of the term similar to the talks that I have been giving to judges and lawyers for almost 40 years. My goal, as in my talks, is to present the cases as clearly as I can and to explain their implications. My hope is to do this in a neutral manner, without evaluating them or editorializing. I certainly have views about many of them and cannot pretend that they do not sometimes affect my presentation of the cases. That is especially true about many of the cases this term—about topics like affirmative action, executive power, and student loan forgiveness, and a First Amendment exemption to antidiscrimination laws. But my goal is to present the cases as fairly as I can and leave my normative judgments to be expressed in other places.

I want to express my great appreciation to my research assistants—Margarita Akopyan, Jordan Barton, Evan Jester, and Allison Klei—for their terrific assistance. And, as always, my wonderful executive assistant, Whitney Mello, was invaluable. Catherine Fisk and Alex Chemerinsky talked through many of the ideas in the book, and Alex provided detailed comments on some of the chapters.

It was another very important term in the Supreme Court, and I feel privileged to have this opportunity to write about it.

1

Introduction: October Term 2022

The 2016 presidential election profoundly reshaped the Supreme Court. President Donald Trump's selection of three justices—Neil Gorsuch, Brett Kavanaugh, and Amy Coney Barrett—created a solid six-justice conservative majority. The impact was seen a year ago in October Term 2021, Justice Barrett's first full term. The Court overruled *Roe v. Wade*,[1] dramatically increased the protection for gun rights,[2] found a First Amendment right for a high-school football coach to pray publicly on the field after games,[3] and ruled that the Environmental Protection Agency lacked the authority to regulate greenhouse gas emissions from coal-fired power plants.[4]

In the last days of October Term 2022, the Court, again in a series of 6–3 decisions, moved the law significantly to the right in restricting affirmative action by colleges and universities,[5] creating a First Amendment exception to state antidiscrimination laws for those engaged in expressive activities,[6] and invalidating President Joe Biden's student loan forgiveness program.[7] But unlike the prior term, there were some significant surprises from the conservative Court, including finding that Alabama violated the Voting Rights Act in its drawing of congressional districts,[8] rejecting the "independent state legislature" theory that would have precluded state courts from enforcing state constitutions in elections for Congress,[9] and upholding the Indian Child Welfare Act.[10] Overall, the conservative position prevailed in the most high-profile cases but less consistently than the year before.

It was also a term where it again seemed to be the John Roberts Court. A year ago, when five justices voted to overrule *Roe v. Wade* without Roberts, some speculated that he had "lost" his Court. But that was generalizing too much for one case, albeit an enormously important one. This term, Chief Justice Roberts wrote the majority opinion in a disproportionate share of the most high-profile cases, including affirmative action,[11] the Voting Rights Act,[12] the independent state legislature theory,[13] and the Biden student loan forgiveness program.[14] He was in the majority in every major case.

But the term's context cannot be ignored in assessing Chief Justice Roberts and the Court. The Court has its lowest approval ratings in history.[15] In June 2023, a Quinnipiac University poll asked 1,800 United States adults about their views on the Supreme Court.[16] The poll showed 35 percent expressing approval of the Supreme Court and 57 percent voicing disapproval.[17] There were serious allegations of ethical improprieties by three justices: Thomas, Gorsuch, and Alito.[18] Despite substantial pressure from various bills, the Court still has not adopted an ethics code. It is inexplicable why all other judges in the country must abide by an ethics code, but not the most powerful and important ones. This matter should not be a partisan issue: an ethics code and an enforcement mechanism would apply to all justices, liberal and conservative.

October Term 2022 by the Numbers

The Supreme Court decided 58 cases with signed opinions after briefing and oral arguments.[19] This number is exactly the same as last year and slightly more than the 54 from two terms earlier or 52 the year before that, which was the smallest number since 1862.[20] It is notable that the Court's docket seems to have stabilized in the 50s range, which is significantly less than even several years ago and radically fewer than the more than 150 cases decided a year in the 1980s.[21] In William Rehnquist's last term as Chief Justice, October Term 2004, the Court decided 80 cases.[22] It has not gotten close to that since John Roberts became Chief Justice.

This year, 47 percent of the cases were decided unanimously,[23] compared with just 29 percent the year before.[24] That, of course, could be a function of the justices consciously trying to achieve consensus, or it may just reflect what matters were on the docket this term. There also were fewer 6–3 decisions this year, 11, compared to 18 the year before.[25] There were another seven that were decided 5–4.[26]

Justice Kavanaugh was the justice most often in the majority, followed by Chief Justice Roberts. In the nonunanimous cases, Kavanaugh was in the majority 90 percent of the time, and Roberts was in the majority of these cases 86 percent of the time.[27]

One clear trend was an increase in the length of oral arguments.[28] When Chief Justice William Rehnquist presided, an advocate had to sit down when the red light came on. Maybe, if fortunate, the lawyer could finish their sentence. But Chief Justice Roberts now allows the arguments to continue as long as the justices have questions. The oral arguments in the affirmative action cases lasted five-and-a-half hours; other cases had oral arguments that lasted more than three hours.

As someone who has argued in the Supreme Court many times, I confess to mixed feelings about this trend. As a lawyer, I always want more time to answer the justices' and the judges' questions. But there also is something reassuring while standing at the podium in knowing that in 30 minutes the red light will come on and I will be able to sit down.

The Supreme Judiciary

What most emerges from reading this term's decisions is that these justices show little deference to others, in or out of the government. From the justices' opinions, there is an overwhelming sense that they believe they know best for the country and feel no need to give much weight to the judgment of others.

There certainly is no deference to the President and the executive branch of government. President Joe Biden provided 43 million individuals with student loans some relief under a federal law that allows the Secretary of Education to "waive or modify" these obligations in an emergency.[29] The Court—in *Biden v. Nebraska,* discussed in Chapter 7—did not dispute whether it was an emergency but said that the statutory authority to "waive" the student loan debt was not sufficiently specific to permit this presidential action.[30]

Nor is there deference to Congress, as the student loan case and others reflect. The Court often has said that once it interprets a statute, Congress can revise the law if it does not like the justices' construction of it. In fact, Justice Brett Kavanaugh said this explicitly this term: "But the *stare decisis* standard for this Court to overrule a statutory precedent, as distinct from a constitutional precedent, is comparatively strict. Unlike with constitutional precedents, Congress and the President may enact new legislation to alter statutory precedents. . . . Although statutory *stare decisis* is not absolute, the Court has ordinarily left the updating or correction of erroneous statutory precedents to the legislative process."[31]

However, the Court abandoned this deference in interpreting Title VII of the 1964 Civil Rights Act, which prohibits employment discrimination based on religion, as well as race or sex. The law requires that employers make reasonable accommodations for employees' religious practices.[32] In 1977, the Court interpreted the law to say that employers do not have to accommodate workers' religious practices if it would impose more than a minimal burden on them.[33] Congress has had 46 years to change that standard and never did.

But in *Groff v. DeJoy*, discussed in Chapter 3, the Court effectively overruled its precedent and changed the legal standard.[34] The Court felt that the earlier approach did not provide enough protection for religious practices and said that employers must accommodate them unless doing so would impose a substantial cost. But shouldn't it have been for Congress to revise the law if it did not like the Court's approach? And how will courts decide what "substantial" means and when employers do and don't have to provide accommodations for employees' religious practices?

The Court likewise showed no deference to state governments. Most states have a law prohibiting business establishments from discriminating based on race, sex, religion, or sexual orientation. They have decided that stopping discrimination is more important than protecting the freedom to discriminate. But the Supreme Court in *303 Creative LLC v. Elenis*, discussed in Chapter 9, held that such laws are unconstitutional when they force a business to serve customers in a way that compels the business to express a message with which it disagrees.[35] As Justice Sotomayor said in her dissent, this was the "first time in its history" that the Court granted "a business open to the public a constitutional right to refuse to serve members of a protected class."[36]

The Court was explicit that it would give no deference to college and university officials—public or private—in their judgment that diversity in the classroom and the campus matters in the education of their students.[37] Over 60 percent of selective colleges and universities engage in affirmative action. They do so because they have judged that diversity is crucial to the education of their students and that there are no other ways to achieve it. In 2003, in *Grutter v. Bollinger*, the Court explicitly spoke of the need to defer to the judgment of university officials.[38] But this term, the Court's majority in *Students for Fair Admission v. President and Trustees of Harvard College*—discussed in Chapter 2—said that it rejected *Grutter*'s deference to educational officials, and schools may no longer use race as one of many factors in admissions to benefit minorities and enhance diversity.[39]

Moreover, the justices give no deference to their predecessors on the Court or to their precedents. We saw this last year when the Court overruled *Roe v. Wade* and again this year in overruling 45 years of precedents allowing affirmative action.

Even in rejecting the independent state legislature theory and ruling that state courts can enforce state constitutions as to elections, Chief Justice Roberts emphasized the role of the federal courts, and thus the Supreme Court, to have the ultimate say. In *Moore v. Harper*, discussed in Chapter 6, Chief Justice Roberts concluded his opinion: "But federal courts must not abandon their own duty to exercise judicial review. In interpreting state law in this area, state courts may not so exceed the bounds of ordinary judicial review as to unconstitutionally intrude upon the role specifically reserved to state legislatures by Article I, Section 4, of the Federal Constitution."[40] It is unclear what this declaration means, but it does give the federal courts—and therefore the Supreme Court—the last word, even as to these matters of state law.

What is apparent is that this is a Court that believes it knows best and feels no compunction to defer to the judgment and wisdom of others. It is unclear what this will mean in the long term. Unquestionably, conservatives who applaud the decisions are untroubled by this, while liberals who decry them are angry and frustrated. But looking through a partisan lens misses the point: it was a term, and we are in a time of the supreme judiciary.

Justice Ketanji Brown Jackson

The Court, of course, had a new justice this year: Ketanji Brown Jackson. She was a federal district court judge for eight years. She and Sonia Sotomayor are the only current justices to have occupied this role, which provides an important perspective as the Supreme Court decides cases that district judges must implement. Jackson spent a year on the United States Court of Appeals for the District of Columbia Circuit before being nominated to replace Justice Stephen Breyer.

Justice Jackson actively participated in oral arguments from her first days on the high-court bench. On the second day of the term, the Court heard oral arguments in *Allen v. Milligan*—discussed in Chapter 6—on applying the Voting Rights Act of 1965 to the drawing of election districts. Justice Jackson left no doubt that she rejected Alabama's claim that the drawing of election districts had to be done in a race-neutral fashion. During the oral arguments she said, "We're talking about a situation in which race has already infused the voting system. So can you help me understand why you think that the world of, you know, race-blind redistricting is really the starting point in this situation?"[41]

During the oral arguments in the affirmative action cases, Justice Jackson made the same powerful point against color blindness when she said: "What I'm worried about is that the rule that you're advocating, that in the context of a holistic review process, the university can take into account and value all of the other background and personal characteristics of other applicants, but they can't value race . . . that seems to me to have the potential of causing more of an equal protection problem than it's actually solving."[42]

Justice Jackson wrote 17 opinions in her first term; six were majority opinions, five were concurring opinions, and six were dissents. I think her two most memorable opinions were dissents. One was in the affirmative action case, *Students for Fair Admission v. President and Trustees of Harvard College*.[43] She began by declaring: "This contention blinks both history and reality in ways too numerous to count. But the response is simple: Our country has never been color-blind. Given the lengthy history of state-sponsored race-based preferences in America, to say that anyone is now victimized if a college considers whether that legacy of discrimination has unequally advantaged its applicants fails to acknowledge the well-documented 'intergenerational transmission of inequality' that still plagues our citizenry."[44] She and Justice Thomas had a sharp disagreement over the desirability of affirmative action and the lessons to draw from America's history of racism. Justice Jackson concluded her dissent: "It would be deeply unfortunate if the Equal Protection Clause actually demanded this perverse, ahistorical, and counterproductive outcome. To impose this result in that Clause's name when it requires no such thing, and to thereby obstruct our collective progress toward the full realization of the Clause's promise, is truly a tragedy for us all."[45]

Her other memorable dissent was in a case that received much less attention, *Jones v. Hendrix*—discussed in Chapter 4—about the availability of habeas corpus for a person who is innocent under the statute but who already had filed one habeas corpus petition.[46] Justice Thomas wrote the opinion for the Court, in a 6–3 decision, precluding habeas relief. Justice Jackson wrote a scathing dissent and lamented: "I am also deeply troubled by the constitutional implications of the nothing-to-see-here approach that the majority takes with respect to the incarceration of potential legal innocents."[47]

She concluded her lengthy dissent by talking more generally about the Court's restrictive approach to habeas corpus and strongly disagreeing with it: "All of these opinions have now collectively managed to transform a statute that Congress designed to provide for a rational and orderly process of federal postconviction judicial review into an aimless and chaotic exercise in futility. The route to obtaining collateral relief is presently replete with imagined artificial barriers, arbitrary dead ends, and traps for the unwary. And today's turn makes the journey palpably absurd."[48]

Although it is a mistake to draw broad conclusions about a justice from one year on the Court, it seems that, as expected, Justice Jackson will be a liberal justice, joining Justices Sotomayor and Kagan when the Court is ideologically divided. She especially will be a strong voice on issues touching race, being the first Black woman and only the third Black individual to ever serve on the Supreme Court. Because she was 51 years old when confirmed for the Court, she will likely be a justice for decades to come.

The Rhetoric

Again, especially in the most high profile cases—affirmative action, Biden's student loan relief, the ability of people to violate antidiscrimination laws on account of their beliefs—there often was sharp rhetoric in the opinions. It was notable therefore that on the last day of the term, in his majority opinion in the student loan case, *Biden v. Nebraska*, Chief Justice Roberts concluded by stating: "It has become a disturbing feature of some recent opinions to criticize the decisions with which they disagree as going beyond the proper role of the judiciary. . . . Reasonable minds may disagree with our analysis—in fact, at least three do. We do not mistake this plainly heartfelt disagreement for disparagement. It is important that the public not be misled either. Any such misperception would be harmful to this institution and our country."[49]

It is notable that Chief Justice Roberts felt the need to say this. In the last two years, the Court has been deciding cases about some of the most divisive and emotional issues confronting American society. It is not surprising that the opinions, especially dissenting ones, express strong feelings. And there have been more instances of justices addressing this in off the bench speeches. Whether any of this will matter for public perceptions of the Court is yet to be known.

Conclusion

October Term 2021 was momentous, from abortion and gun rights to religion and greenhouse gas emissions. In the past, the Court seemed to follow a blockbuster term with a sleepier one. October Term 2022 deviated from this pattern. As described in the following chapters, it was another momentous year—filled with cases that significantly changed the law in many areas and that will significantly affect people's lives.

Endnotes

1. Dobbs v. Jackson Women's Health Org., 142 S. Ct. 2228, 2242 (2022).
2. New York State Rifle & Pistol Ass'n, Inc. v. Bruen, 142 S. Ct. 2111, 2156 (2022).
3. Kennedy v. Bremerton Sch. Dist., 142 S. Ct. 2407, 2415 (2022).
4. W. Virginia v. Env't Prot. Agency, 213 L. Ed. 2d 896, 142 S. Ct. 2587, 2616 (2022).
5. Students for Fair Admissions, Inc. v. President & Fellows of Harvard Coll., 143 S. Ct. 2141 (2023).
6. Creative LLC v. Elenis, 143 S. Ct. 2298 (2023).
7. Biden v. Nebraska, 143 S. Ct. 2355 (2023).
8. Allen v. Milligan, 143 S. Ct. 1487, 1498 (2023).
9. Moore v. Harper, 143 S. Ct. 2065 (2023).
10. Haaland v. Brackeen, 143 S. Ct. 1609, 1641 (2023).
11. Students for Fair Admissions, Inc. v. President & Fellows of Harvard Coll., 143 S. Ct. 2141 (2023).
12. Allen v. Milligan, 143 S. Ct. 1487, 1498 (2023).
13. Moore v. Harper, 143 S. Ct. 2065 (2023).
14. Biden v. Nebraska, 143 S. Ct. 2355 (2023).
15. *Supreme Court*, GALLUP (2023), https://news.gallup.com/poll/4732/supreme-court.aspx.
16. Joseph Konig, *Americans' view of the Supreme Court at near two-decade low*, SPECTRUM NEWS NY (May 25, 2023, 7:00 PM), https://www.ny1.com/nyc/all-boroughs/politics/2023/05/25/supreme-court-approval-rating-low-poll.
17. *Id.*
18. *See, e.g.*, Nina Totenberg, *Clarence Thomas, Samuel Alito and the crisis of confidence in the Supreme Court*, NPR: MORNING EDITION (June 28, 2023, 5:06 AM), https://www.npr.org/2023/06/28/1183337280/supreme-court-ethics-financial-disclosures-possible-conflicts-of-interest.

19. *Opinions of the Court—2022*, U.S. (2023), https://www.supremecourt.gov/opinions/slipopinion/22.

20. *Id.*

21. *See e.g.*, 444 U.S. (1980): 445 U.S. (1980); 446 U.S. (1980); 447 U.S. (1980); 448 U.S. (1980); 449 U.S. (1980).

22. 543 U.S. (2004); 544 U.S. (2004); 545 U.S. (2004).

23. Adam Liptak, *Along with Conservative Triumphs, Signs of New Caution at Supreme Court*, NEW YORK TIMES (July 1, 2023), https://www.nytimes.com/2023/07/01/us/supreme-court-liberal-conservative.html.

24. Angie Gou, *As unanimity declines, conservative majority's power runs deeper than the blockbuster cases*, SCOTUSBLOG (July 3, 2023, 8:21 PM), https://www.scotusblog.com/2022/07/as-unanimity-declines-conservative-majoritys-power-runs-deeper-than-the-blockbuster-cases/.

25. Jake Trustcott, *Another One Bites the Dust: End of 2022/2023 Supreme Court Statistics*, EMPIRICAL SCOTUS (June 30, 2023), https://empiricalscotus.com/2023/06/30/another-one-bites-2022/.

26. *Id.*

27. Liptak, *supra* note 23.

28. Trustcott, *supra* note 25.

29. WAIVER AUTHORITY OR RESPONSE TO MILITARY CONTINGENCIES AND NATIONAL EMERGENCIES, 20 U.S.C.§ 1098bb.

30. Biden v. Nebraska, 143 S. Ct. 2355 (2023).

31. Allen v. Milligan, 143 S. Ct. 1487, 1517 (2023) (Kavanaugh, J., concurring).

32. CIVIL RIGHTS ACT, 42 U.S.C. § 2000e(j).

33. Trans World Airlines, Inc. v. Hardison, 432 U.S. 63 (1977).

34. 143 S. Ct. 2279 (2023).

35. 143 S. Ct. 2298 (2023).

36. *Id.* at 2322 (Sotomayor, J., dissenting).

37. Students for Fair Admissions, Inc. v. President & Fellows of Harvard Coll., 143 S. Ct. 2141 (2023).

38. Grutter v. Bollinger, 123 S. Ct. 2325, 2339 (2003).

39. Students for Fair Admissions, Inc. v. President & Fellows of Harvard Coll., 143 S. Ct. 2141 (2023).

40. 143 S. Ct. 2065, 2090 (2023).

41. Caroline Sullivan, *Three Takeaways: Merrill v. Milligan Oral Arguments*, DEMOCRACY DOCKET (October 5, 2022), https://www.democracydocket.com/analysis/three-takeaways-merrill-v-milligan-oral-arguments/.

42. Joanna Walters and Edwin Rios, *Ketanji Brown Jackson grills lawyer in case seeking to end affirmative action*, THE GUARDIAN (Nov. 1, 2022, 1:04 PM), https://www.theguardian.com/law/2022/nov/01/ketanji-brown-jackson-affirmative-action-higher-education-admissions.

43. Justice Jackson actually was recused from the Harvard case, likely because she had recently been on the Harvard Board of Overseers. But she participated in the North Carolina case, and both were decided in the same opinion.

44. 143 S. Ct. 2141, 2264 (Jackson, J., dissenting).

45. *Id.* at 2279.

46. 143 S. Ct. 1857 (2023).

47. 143 S. Ct. at 1878.

48. *Id.* at 1898.

49. 143 S. Ct. at 2375–76.

2

Affirmative Action

No cases received more attention in October Term 2022 than *Students for Fair Admission v. University of North Carolina* and *Students for Fair Admission v. President and Fellows of Harvard College*. The issue was whether colleges and universities may continue to use race as a factor in admissions decisions to benefit minorities and enhance diversity. In a 6–3 decision, with the majority opinion written by Chief John Roberts, the Court emphatically said no, implicitly overruling 45 years of precedent and leaving open many questions about what colleges and universities may do to achieve diversity.

Past Precedents

The Court first considered the issue of affirmative action in *Regents of the University of California v. Bakke*.[1] *Bakke* involved a challenge to the University of California at Davis Medical School's policy of setting aside 16 slots in the entering class of 100 for minority students. There was no majority opinion for the Supreme Court. Four Justices—Brennan, White, Marshall, and Blackmun— said that intermediate scrutiny was the appropriate test for racial classifications benefiting minorities. They said that "a number of considerations . . . lead us to conclude that racial classifications designed to further remedial purposes must serve important governmental objectives and must be substantially related to achievement of those objectives."[2] These four Justices voted to uphold the University of California at Davis Medical School's affirmative action program.

Four Justices—Stevens, Burger, Stewart, and Rehnquist—concluded that the affirmative action program violated Title VI of the 1964 Civil Rights Act, which prohibited discrimination by institutions receiving federal funds. They did not reach the constitutional issue or discuss the level of scrutiny. However, five Justices—Brennan, White, Marshall, Blackmun, and Powell—rejected this view and concluded that the analysis under Title VI and the Constitution is identical. That remains the law and was crucial to the Court's holding that the Harvard College affirmative action plan was impermissible.

Finally, Justice Powell, writing just for himself, said that strict scrutiny should be used for affirmative action. He said that "[r]acial and ethnic distinctions of any sort are inherently suspect and thus call for the most exacting judicial examination."[3] Powell concluded that the set-aside was unconstitutional but that it was permissible for race to be used as one factor in admissions decisions to enhance diversity. Thus, the vote was 5 to 4 invalidating the set-aside—Powell, Stevens, Burger, Rehnquist, and Stewart voting for this conclusion—but 5 to 4 that it is permissible for universities to use race as a factor in admissions to increase diversity—Powell, Brennan, Marshall, White, and Blackmun coming to this conclusion.

The Supreme Court returned to the issue of affirmative action in higher education a quarter century later. In *Grutter v. Bollinger (2003)*, in a 5–4 decision, with Justice Sandra Day O'Connor writing for the majority, the Court upheld the University of Michigan Law School's affirmative action program.[4] The Court ruled that colleges and universities have a compelling interest in creating a diverse student body and that they may use race as one factor, among many, to benefit minorities and enhance diversity. The Court said that the "benefits [of diversity] are substantial" and diversity "promotes cross-racial understanding, helps to break down racial stereotypes, and enables students to better understand persons of different races."[5]

The Court accepted the university's argument that the education of all students is enhanced with a diverse student body. In other words, a majority of the Court adopted Justice Powell's approach from *Bakke*.

Finally, in *Fisher v. University of Texas at Austin*, in 2016, the Court reaffirmed these holdings.[6] Initially, the justices held that for an affirmative action program to be upheld, the college or university must prove that no less discriminatory alternative can achieve diversity.[7] After a remand to the federal court of appeals, the Court concluded that Texas met this burden.

The Supreme Court's decision was 4–3. Justice Scalia died after the oral argument and before the decision. Justice Kagan was recused, likely because of her involvement with the case as Solicitor General of the United States. Justice Kennedy wrote for the Court.

Justice Kennedy concluded his majority opinion—which was the first time he ever had voted to uphold an affirmative action program—by expressing the need for deference to colleges and universities. He wrote: "Considerable deference is owed to a university in defining those intangible characteristics, like student body diversity, that are central to its identity and educational mission. But still, it remains an enduring challenge to our Nation's education system to reconcile the pursuit of diversity with the constitutional promise of equal treatment and dignity. In striking this sensitive balance, public universities, like the States themselves, can serve as 'laboratories for experimentation.'"[8]

Students for Fair Admission v. President and Regents of Harvard College and *Students for Fair Admission v. University of North Carolina*

Thus, the law prior to June 2023 was clear: The Court held that colleges and universities have a compelling interest in having a diverse student body and they may use race as one factor in admissions to benefit minorities and enhance diversity. However, they could not have a quota, set-aside, or add additional points to applications from minority races.

Just seven years after the Court's decision in *Fisher* upholding affirmative action, the issue was back before the Supreme Court as to whether to overrule these precedents and declare affirmative action unconstitutional. What changed in that relatively short time? The composition of the Court. All three dissenters in *Fisher*—Chief Justice Roberts and Justices Thomas and Alito—remained on the Court. Since 2016, they were joined by Justices Gorsuch, Kavanaugh, and Barrett. These six justices were the majority in a 6–3 decision to effectively overrule the earlier precedent and hold that colleges and universities cannot use race as a factor in admissions decisions to benefit minorities.

Both cases were brought by the same plaintiff, Students for Fair Admissions. The suit against the University of North Carolina contends that the school's affirmative action program violates equal protection. A federal district court held an eight-day trial and then ruled in favor of the University of North Carolina, concluding that, in accordance with Supreme Court precedent, it used race as one factor among many in admissions and that it did not have another way to achieve diversity. The Supreme Court granted review before the case could be heard and decided by the United States Court of Appeals for the Fourth Circuit.

The suit against Harvard College claims that it violates Title VI of the 1964 Civil Rights Act, which prohibits racial discrimination by recipients of federal funds. The equal protection clause and the Constitution do not apply to Harvard because it is a private institution. The plaintiffs contend that Harvard discriminates against Asian students in its admissions policies. A federal district court judge held a 15-day trial and ruled in favor of Harvard. The court concluded that Harvard did not intentionally discriminate against Asian Americans and that it used race as a factor in admissions because it is necessary in order to have diversity in its student body. The United States Court of Appeals for the First Circuit affirmed and found that the Harvard program did not violate Title VI.

Although the two cases involve different claims, one constitutional and the other statutory, as described above, the Supreme Court previously had said that the legal standard is the same under Title VI and under equal protection. The effect of the Court taking both cases is that it resolved the future of affirmative action at both public and private universities.

Both cases were decided under the title, *Students for Fair Admissions v. President and Fellows of Harvard College.*[9] Chief Justice Roberts wrote for the Court, which was expected. Since coming on the bench in 2005, he has been a strong foe of affirmative action programs.[10] The North Carolina case was 6–3, while the Harvard case was 6–2 because Justice Jackson was recused as she had recently been on the Harvard Board of Overseers.

Chief Justice Roberts' majority opinion was explicit that colleges and universities cannot engage in affirmative action. The Court declared: "University programs must comply with strict scrutiny, they may never use race as a stereotype or negative, and—at some point—they must end. Respondents' admissions systems—however well intentioned and implemented in good faith—fail each of these criteria. They must therefore be invalidated under the Equal Protection Clause of the Fourteenth Amendment."[11]

While the earlier cases had ruled that diversity is a compelling government interest, the Court expressly rejected this interest as insufficient to meet strict scrutiny. The Court found diversity too amorphous an objective to be deemed compelling. Whereas the earlier cases had expressed the need for deference to college and universities, the Court rejected such deference. Chief Justice Roberts stated: "Universities may define their missions as they see fit. The Constitution defines ours. Courts may not license separating students on the basis of race without an exceedingly persuasive justification that is measurable and concrete enough to permit judicial review."[12]

The Court said that giving a preference to some based on race means that others are disadvantaged because of their race and that is inconsistent with the Constitution's guarantee of equal protection. Chief Justice Roberts concluded the majority opinion by declaring: "For the reasons provided above, the Harvard and UNC admissions programs cannot be reconciled with the guarantees of the Equal Protection Clause. Both programs lack sufficiently focused and measurable objectives warranting the use of race, unavoidably employ race in a negative manner, involve racial stereotyping, and lack meaningful end points. We have never permitted admissions programs to work in that way, and we will not do so today."[13]

There were three concurring opinions, with the longest by Justice Clarence Thomas. He recited the history of race discrimination in the United States and of the Fourteenth Amendment and concluded from it that the Constitution should be read as requiring color blindness. He said that he wrote "separately to offer an originalist defense of the colorblind Constitution; to explain further the flaws of the Court's *Grutter* jurisprudence; to clarify that all forms of discrimination based on race—including so-called affirmative action—are prohibited under the Constitution; and to emphasize the pernicious effects of all such discrimination."[14] Justice Thomas had vehemently dissented in *Grutter* and in every case approving affirmative action since coming on the Court in 1991. Now he was in the majority in overruling those decisions.

Justice Gorsuch wrote separately to stress that affirmative action violates Title VI, the federal law which prohibits recipients of federal funds from discriminating based on race.[15] Since virtually all universities—private and public—receive federal funds, the reach of the Court's holding is large.

Justice Kavanaugh also concurred and stressed, as did Chief Justice Roberts' majority opinion, that the Court in *Grutter* always intended that there would be an end to affirmative action. Justice O'Connor's opinion suggested 25 years. Justice Kavanaugh wrote to say that the time had come and that this decision was consistent with what the Court had in mind in 2003 when *Grutter* was decided.

Both Justice Sotomayor and Justice Jackson wrote vehement dissents, each joined by the other and by Justice Kagan. Justice Sotomayor lamented the overruling of decades of precedents and of the Court keeping colleges and universities from acting to advance racial equality. She wrote: "the Court cements a superficial rule of colorblindness as a constitutional principle in an endemically segregated society where race has always mattered and continues to matter. The Court subverts the constitutional guarantee of equal protection by further entrenching racial inequality in education, the very foundation of our democratic government and pluralistic society."[16]

Justice Sotomayor said that the decision would have a "devastating impact" on enrollment of students of color. She concluded her dissent: "Today, this Court overrules decades of precedent and imposes a superficial rule of race blindness on the Nation. The devastating impact of this decision cannot be overstated. The majority's vision of race neutrality will entrench racial segregation in higher education because racial inequality will persist so long as it is ignored."[17]

Justice Jackson also wrote a strong dissenting opinion. She focused on two fictional students throughout her dissent: John, a white student who is the seventh generation in his family to go to the University of North Carolina, and James, a Black student who is the first in his family to go to college. She used these examples to illustrate that the legacy of slavery and discrimination have enormous current effects. She wrote: "Our country has never been color-blind. Given the lengthy history of state-sponsored race-based preferences in America, to say that anyone is now victimized if a college considers whether that legacy of discrimination has unequally advantaged its applicants fails to acknowledge the well-documented 'intergenerational transmission of inequality' that still plagues our citizenry."[18] She spoke of the tremendous racial inequalities in American society, in education and by every measure. She concluded her dissent: "It would be deeply unfortunate if the Equal Protection Clause actually demanded this perverse, ahistorical, and counterproductive outcome. To impose this result in that Clause's name when it requires no such thing, and to thereby obstruct our collective progress toward the full realization of the Clause's promise, is truly a tragedy for us all."[19]

The Differing Perspectives of the Majority and the Dissents

There are fundamental differences between the justices in the majority and the justices in the dissent, reflecting the deep social divide on the subject of affirmative action. First, the majority and the dissent strenuously disagree about whether using race to benefit minorities should be thought of the same way as using race to the detriment of people of color. For the majority, any use of race is unacceptable. When the government uses race as a factor to help some, it is hurting others and the majority sees that as always wrong. For the dissent, there is a profound difference between using race to subordinate racial minorities and using race to benefit minorities and enhance diversity in the context of a society with a long and continuing legacy of race discrimination.

Second, there is great disagreement over whether diversity in classrooms and in campuses should be regarded as a compelling interest. The majority expressly rejects this and the precedents that had approved it. But the dissent expressly defends diversity as being essential to the education of all students.

Third, there is great disagreement between the majority and the dissent over the lessons of history. Almost all of the opinions described the tragic history of race discrimination from the earliest days of American history. The majority opinion and the concurrence of Justice Thomas see the history as justifying their conclusion that the Constitution requires color blindness. But the dissenting justices look at history as justifying the use of race to remedy past discrimination and enhance diversity. They see a commitment to color blindness as preventing essential steps towards racial equality.

What Will It Mean?

Although the Court did not expressly say it was overruling *Bakke*, *Grutter*, and *Fisher*, there is no doubt that is exactly what the Court did. Every concurring and dissenting opinion described it this way. It will mean that colleges and universities cannot use race as a factor in admissions decisions to benefit minorities and enhance diversity.

There likely will be an immediate detrimental effect on admission of students of color at selective colleges and universities. This was the experience in states like California and Michigan that have already abolished affirmative action by voter initiative. In 1996, California voters passed Proposition 209, which provides that governments in California cannot discriminate or give preference based on race or sex in education, contracting, or employment. Justice Sotomayor in her dissent described the impact: "The decline was particularly devastating at California's most selective campuses, where the rates of admission of underrepresented groups 'dropped by 50% or more.' At the University of California, Berkeley, a top public university not just in California but also nationally, the percentage of Black students in the freshman class dropped from 6.32% in 1995 to 3.37% in 1998. Latino representation similarly dropped from 15.57% to 7.28% during that period at Berkeley, even though Latinos represented 31% of California public high school graduates. . . . For example, as of 2019, the proportion of Black freshmen at Berkeley was 2.76%, well below the pre-constitutional amendment level in 1996, which was 6.32%. Latinos composed about 15% of freshmen students at Berkeley in 2019, despite making up 52% of all California public high school graduates."[20] It took UCLA 19 years after Proposition 209 was enacted, until 2015, to achieve its pre-1996 levels of student diversity.

A great deal will depend on what colleges and universities will be able to do in order to achieve diversity. The Court held that colleges and universities cannot give preference based on race, but it did not keep them from pursuing diversity through race-neutral means.

For example, nothing in the opinion precludes colleges and universities from engaging in outreach to encourage diverse students to apply or to enroll once accepted. Enhancing the pipeline of qualified students of color will be imperative. The admissions process for schools involves three major steps: encouraging students to apply, admissions decisions, and persuading admitted students to attend. The Court's decision focuses on the middle step but does not speak to targeted outreach or recruitment.

Additionally, Chief Justice Roberts suggested that there were ways in which colleges and universities could continue to consider race. He wrote: "nothing in this opinion should be construed as prohibiting universities from considering an applicant's discussion of how race affected his or her life, be it through discrimination, inspiration, or otherwise."[21] But this would seem to be a challenge for admissions offices and for courts reviewing their programs. No preference could be given based on race, but race could be used as a positive if it was about overcoming adversity. Chief Justice Roberts qualified this: "But, despite the dissent's assertion to the contrary, universities may not simply establish through application essays or other means the regime we hold unlawful today. [W]hat cannot be done directly cannot be done indirectly. . . . A benefit to a student who overcame racial discrimination, for example, must be tied to *that student's* courage and determination. Or a benefit to a student whose heritage or culture motivated him or her to assume a leadership role or attain a particular goal must be tied to *that student's* unique ability to contribute to the university. In other words, the student must be treated based on his or her experiences as an individual—not on the basis of race."[22]

It is unclear what this will mean in practice. A college or university cannot give a preference based on race, but it can take into account how a student overcame racial discrimination or how his or her race was an inspiration. This seems a difficult line to draw, both for the schools and ultimately for the courts when there are legal challenges.

Lastly, it is unclear if colleges and universities can use race-neutral proxies to achieve diversity. For example, the University of Texas created a program of accepting the top 10 percent of high schools in the state. Texas is sufficiently racially segregated that this would yield some degree of diversity. Is this permissible because it is facially race neutral? Or is this unconstitutional because it is done with the purpose of benefiting minorities and it has that effect?

Conclusion

I doubt that anyone was surprised by the Court's decision to end affirmative action. Conservatives have long and vehemently opposed race conscious admissions programs. The conservative justices have bitterly dissented from earlier rulings allowing affirmative action. With six conservative justices, it seemed inevitable that the Court would overrule *Bakke*, *Grutter*, and *Fisher.* Now that it has happened, the focus needs to be on what schools still can do to achieve diversity. Some schools likely will move aggressively to find alternative ways to ensure diversity, while other schools probably will do much less. There surely will be a great deal of litigation clarifying what is permissible and impermissible in light of these efforts. The Court's decision in *Students for Fair Admission v. Harvard College* is enormously important but hardly the last word on schools' efforts to achieve diversity. It also is unclear whether the Court's decision is a harbinger of other likely changes in the law, such as reconsidering affirmative action programs in employment under Title VII of the 1964 Civil Rights Act.

Endnotes

1. 438 U.S. 265 (1978).
2. *Id.* at 359 (citations omitted).
3. *Id.* at 291.
4. 539 U.S. 306 (2003).
5. 539 U.S. at 330.

6. 579 U.S. 365 (2016).
7. 570 U.S. 297, 311 (2013).
8. 579 U.S. at 387–88.
9. 143 S. Ct. 2141 (2023).
10. *See* JOAN BISKUPIC, THE LIFE AND TURBULENT TIMES OF JOHN ROBERTS 97–100, 133–134 (2019).
11. 143 S. Ct. at 2166.
12. *Id.* at 2168.
13. *Id.* at 2175.
14. *Id.* at 2177 (Thomas, J., concurring).
15. *Id.* at 2208 (Gorsuch, J., concurring).
16. *Id.* at 2226 (Sotomayor, J., dissenting).
17. *Id.* at 2263.
18. *Id.* at 2264 (Jackson, J., dissenting).
19. *Id.* at 2279.
20. *Id.* at 2260 (Sotomayor, J., dissenting).
21. *Id.* at 2176.
22. *Id.*

3

Civil Rights Statutes

In addition to an important decision about the Voting Rights Act, considered in the Chapter 6, there were two important cases about other civil rights statutes. One involved the question of when there can be a lawsuit under 42 U.S.C. § 1983 to enforce federal laws adopted by Congress under its spending power. The other concerned the standard to be used for determining what an employer must do to provide reasonable accommodation for an employee's religious practices to avoid liability for discrimination under Title VII. In the former, the Court reaffirmed precedent and did not change the law, but in the latter case, the Court effectively overruled a 45-year-old decision and created a new test that is likely to spawn a great deal of litigation.

Health and Hospital Corporation of Marion County v. Talevski

There are many federal laws that appropriate money and impose conditions on recipients but do not contain an enforcement mechanism other than the cutting of federal government funds. In other words, the laws don't authorize lawsuits to enforce the requirements imposed by federal law.

In *Maine v. Thiboutot*, in 1980, the Court held that plaintiffs may sue under 42 U.S.C. § 1983 to enforce federal laws adopted under the spending clause.[1] The plaintiffs filed suit in state court against the state of Maine and its officers, alleging that they had violated federal statutory provisions concerning the calculation of welfare benefits. The state argued that there was no cause of action under § 1983 because that statute was available only to remedy violations of statutes protecting civil rights. The Supreme Court, in *Thiboutot*, rejected these arguments. The Court concluded that under the literal language of the statute, § 1983 suits are available whenever any federal law has been allegedly violated. The Court stated: "The question before us is whether the phrase 'and laws,' as used in § 1983, means what it says or whether it should be limited to some subset of laws. Given that Congress attached no modifiers to the phrase, the plain language of the statute undoubtedly embraces respondents' claim that petitioners violated the Social Security Act."[2]

In subsequent cases, the Supreme Court made such suits more difficult.[3] First, § 1983 may not be used to enforce statutes that explicitly or implicitly preclude § 1983 litigation. Second, § 1983 is available only to enforce federal statutes that create rights. A body of case law developed as to each of these exceptions, but still the general principle established by *Maine v. Thiboutot* remained: Section 1983 can be used to enforce federal spending laws.

In *Health and Hospital Corporation of Marion County v. Talevski*,[4] the Court was asked to overrule *Maine v. Thiboutot* and end such litigation. The case involved a lawsuit brought on behalf of a patient in a county-owned nursing home claiming that its treatment of the patient violated rights guaranteed to him under the Federal Nursing Home Reform Act.

The Act requires that nursing homes that receive Medicaid funding respect and protect their residents' health, safety, and dignity. The law refers to the rights of nursing-home residents to be free from unnecessary physical or chemical restraints and to be discharged or transferred only when certain preconditions are satisfied. It is a law adopted by Congress under its spending power.

The Supreme Court, in an opinion by Justice Ketanji Brown Jackson, expressly reaffirmed *Maine v. Thiboutot* and held that laws adopted under the spending clause can be enforced through § 1983 suits. Moreover, the Court said that the Federal Nursing Home Reform Act creates enforceable rights and thus can be the basis for suits under § 1983. Justice Jackson concluded the majority opinion by declaring: "§ 1983 is available to enforce every right that Congress validly and unambiguously creates; we will not impose a categorical font-of-power condition that the Reconstruction Congress did not. And, here, the test that our precedents establish leads inexorably to the conclusion that the FNHRA secures the particular rights that Talevski invokes."[5]

Justice Clarence Thomas wrote a dissenting opinion urging the overruling of *Maine v. Thiboutot*, while Justice Samuel Alito wrote a dissent urging the narrowing of the ability to sue under § 1983 to enforce spending clause laws. Also, Justice Neil Gorsuch wrote an enigmatic concurring opinion raising the question of whether forcing states to comply with the federal spending clause requirements is impermissibly commandeering them in violation of the Tenth Amendment.

But the bottom line is that the Court preserved an important tool of civil rights litigation. When the Court granted review in *Tavleski*, there was concern that it would preclude § 1983 suits to enforce federal laws that had been adopted by Congress under its spending power. The Court did not do that or change the law that had developed in this area.

Groff v. DeJoy

Title VII of the 1964 Civil Rights Act prohibits employment discrimination based on race, sex, or religion. With regard to religion, it creates liability for employers "to fail or refuse to hire or to discharge any individual, or otherwise to discriminate against any individual with respect to his compensation, terms, conditions, or privileges [of] employment, because of such individual's . . . religion." The Equal Employment Opportunity Commission interpreted this to mean that employers must make "reasonable accommodations to the religious needs of employees" whenever that would not work an "undue hardship on the conduct of the employer's business." The crucial questions then are what constitutes "reasonable accommodations" and what is an "undue hardship."

In *Trans World Airlines, Inc. v. Hardison*, the Supreme Court articulated the standard for determining this.[6] It said that employers do not have to bear more than a "*de minimis* cost" to accommodate employees' religious practices. In other words, if it is more than a minimal cost to the employer, its failure to provide an accommodation does not violate Title VII.

In *Groff v. DeJoy*, the Court rejected this standard and adopted a new one, which is much more protective of religious freedom. Gerald Groff works for the United States Postal Service. He is an Evangelical Christian who says that his religion requires that he use his Sunday Sabbath for worship and rest. After USPS entered into an agreement with Amazon to do Sunday deliveries, a work schedule was developed for workers. Groff was among those who was told that he would need to work on Sundays on a rotating basis.

USPS found others to work on Sundays instead of Groff, but "Groff continued to receive 'progressive discipline' for failing to work on Sundays." In January 2019, he resigned and then sued USPS under Title VII. The lower courts ruled against Groff, using the standard from *TWA v. Hardison* and concluded that accommodating Groff's religious beliefs would impose more than a minimal burden on USPS.

The Supreme Court in a unanimous decision reversed the lower courts. Justice Alito wrote for the Court. The Court stated: "We hold that showing 'more than a *de minimis* cost,' as that phrase is used in common parlance, does not suffice to establish 'undue hardship' under Title VII."[7] This is a clear rejection of the standard that has been followed for the last 45 years under *TWA v. Hardison*.

But the question then becomes: what is the new legal standard? The Court declared: "We think it is enough to say that an employer must show that the burden of granting an accommodation would result in substantial increased costs in relation to the conduct of its particular business. What matters more than a favored synonym for 'undue hardship' (which is the actual text) is that courts must apply the test in a manner that takes into account all relevant factors in the case at hand, including the particular accommodations at issue and their practical impact in light of the nature, 'size and operating cost of [an] employer.'"[8]

The Court says no more than this in explaining this standard or what it means. Employers do not have to provide accommodations for employees' religious beliefs if doing so would impose a "substantial cost." The crucial issue will be how courts are to decide what is an insubstantial cost, so that employers must provide the accommodation, or is a substantial cost so that they don't. For that the Court gives little guidance to lower courts and litigants.

The Court stresses the burden on employers to accommodate employees' religious beliefs, including to consider alternative ways to do this. Justice Alito says that "Title VII requires that an employer reasonably accommodate an employee's practice of religion, not merely that it assess the reasonableness of a particular possible accommodation or accommodations. This distinction matters. Faced with an accommodation request like Groff's, it would not be enough for an employer to conclude that forcing other employees to work overtime would constitute an undue hardship. Consideration of other options, such as voluntary shift swapping, would also be necessary."[9]

But it undoubtedly will take much litigation for the Court to clarify how its new standard is to be applied and how it is to be determined what is a substantial cost in the totality of the circumstances.

Justice Sotomayor, joined by Justice Jackson, wrote a concurring opinion to stress that "[b]ecause the 'conduct of [a] business' plainly includes the management and performance of the business's employees, undue hardship on the conduct of a business may include undue hardship on the business's employees. There is no basis in the text of the statute, let alone in economics or common sense, to conclude otherwise. Indeed, for many businesses, labor is more important to the conduct of the business than any other factor. [I]f there is an undue hardship on 'the conduct of the employer's business,' then such hardship is sufficient, even if it consists of hardship on employees."[10]

The bottom line is that the Court is providing much more protection for the religious practices of employees and a greater ability to sue under Title VII when accommodations are not provided. The Court has changed the standard that has been followed since 1977 and there is now a new legal test to be used in these cases. This is sure to spawn a large increase in claims of religious discrimination and requests for religious accommodation, some of which will lead to litigation.

Endnotes

1. 448 U.S. 1 (1980).
2. *Id.* at 4.
3. The law concerning these exceptions is reviewed in ERWIN CHEMERINSKY, FEDERAL JURISDICTION, chapter 8 (8th ed. 2020).
4. 143 S. Ct. 1444 (2023).
5. *Id.* at 1462.
6. 432 U.S. 63, 84 (1977).
7. 143 S. Ct. at 2294.
8. *Id.* at 2295.
9. *Id.* at 2296–97.
10. *Id.* at 2298 (Sotomayor, J., dissenting).

4

Criminal Law and Procedure

Again, this term, the Supreme Court did not decide cases about the Fourth Amendment or the Fifth Amendment privilege against self-incrimination. There were important criminal cases, but once more, none were blockbusters. In part, this might reflect that Congress is adopting few new criminal laws that would require clarification from the Supreme Court. In part, too, it reflects a trend that has been largely overlooked: the Court is taking very few cases reviewing state court decisions. In October Term 2022, of the 58 cases decided with signed opinions after briefing and oral argument, only five reviewed state court decisions. Because most criminal prosecutions are in state court, this trend limits the likelihood of criminal procedure issues being decided. Also, it does not seem that the Roberts Court "agenda" is about criminal law and procedure. That said, there were several significant cases in this area.

Jones v. Hendrix: Habeas Corpus

Jones v. Hendrix continues the trend of the Supreme Court restricting the availability of habeas corpus by narrowly interpreting provisions of the Antiterrorism and Effective Death Penalty Act (AEDPA).[1] It was a 6–3 decision, with Justice Thomas writing the opinion, and Justices Sotomayor and Jackson writing vehement dissents.

In 2000, the United States District Court for the Western District of Missouri sentenced Marcus DeAngelo Jones to 27 years in prison for two counts of possession of a firearm as a felon.[2] He appealed, and the sentence was affirmed.[3] He later filed a motion to vacate his sentence, pursuant to a 28 U.S.C. § 2255 motion.[4] The district court denied his motion, but the Eighth Circuit reversed, concluding that Jones had ineffective counsel and that he should never have received two duplicate charges.[5] Jones was resentenced, removing one count of possession of a firearm and resolving his § 2255 motion.[6]

Before 1948, federal prisoners could collaterally attack their convictions through habeas corpus petitions filed in the district where they were imprisoned.[7] This led to a flood of petitions in districts with federal prisons and difficulties, as the new court was unfamiliar with the underlying facts and disconnected from the relevant evidence and witnesses.[8] In 1948, Congress passed 28 U.S.C § 2255, creating a new process in which federal prisoners now file their petitions in their sentencing court.[9] Under 28 U.S.C § 2255, Congress included clause (e), or the "saving clause," stipulating that habeas petitions would no longer be permitted unless the remedy by motion is "inadequate or ineffective to test the legality" of detention.[10] This clause is key to *Jones v. Hendrix*, and the ruling mainly hinges on Congress's intent behind the saving clause.

Congress subsequently passed the Anti-Terrorism and Effective Death Penalty Act of 1996. Enacted in the wake of the Oklahoma City bombing, AEDPA bars "second or successive" § 2255 motions, with exceptions for newly discovered evidence or a new rule of constitutional law made retroactive by the Supreme Court.[11] There is no mention of statutory legal innocence claims.[12]

In *Rehaif v. United States*, the Supreme Court said that the charge of possession of a firearm by a felon required the government to prove that the defendants knew both that they possessed a firearm and that they were prohibited from doing so.[13] The second element was never proven at Jones' trial, meaning that Jones has a claim for his legal innocence: a crucial element of his crime was never proven.[14]

But Jones already filed his one § 2255 motion, and AEDPA bars him from bringing another.[15] Jones filed a habeas petition arguing that his inability to bring another motion to vacate meant that § 2255 was "inadequate or ineffective," and he, therefore, could file for habeas corpus under § 2241.[16]

In a 6–3 decision, divided along ideological lines, the Supreme Court ruled against Jones, holding that the saving clause in § 2255(e) does not allow a prisoner asserting an intervening change in the interpretation of a criminal statute to circumvent AEDPA's restrictions on second § 2255 motions by filing a habeas petition under § 2241.[17] Justice Thomas saw the use of the savings clause as a circumvention, or an "end-run," around the limits created by AEDPA.[18] Because AEDPA carved out two specific exceptions to the bar on successive § 2255 motions—for newly discovered facts and for changes in the law that the Supreme Court says apply retroactively—Thomas said that the bar against successive petitions applies to previously unavailable statutory claims.[19]

Justice Thomas read the saving clause very narrowly, arguing that Congress intended AEDPA as a filter to limit habeas claims excepting only highly unusual circumstances, such as if the sentencing court no longer exists.[20] He argued that any other view of the saving clause would make AEDPA "self-defeating" based on the Congressional purpose of limiting successive § 2255 motions.[21] Thomas wrote that "[t]he inability of a prisoner with a statutory claim to satisfy those conditions does not mean that he can bring his claim in a habeas petition under the saving clause. It means that he cannot bring it at all. Congress has chosen finality over error correction in his case."[22]

Justice Sotomayor, joined by Justice Kagan, dissented and pointed to the unfairness of not allowing a habeas petition in these circumstances. She wrote, "A prisoner who is actually innocent, imprisoned for conduct that Congress did not criminalize, is forever barred by 28 U.S.C. § 2255(h) from raising that claim, merely because he previously sought postconviction relief. It does not matter that an intervening decision of this Court confirms his innocence. By challenging his conviction once before, he forfeited his freedom."[23]

Justice Jackson wrote a vehement dissent, disagreeing with the Court's reasoning and conclusion and strongly disapproving of its approach to habeas corpus.[24] In an exhaustive history of the context and Congressional intent behind § 2255, Jackson argued that the statute was only ever meant to resolve a practical problem while preserving the types of claims already available via habeas, not to narrow the potential for postconviction relief.[25] She said that § 2255(e) was meant to literally "save" habeas claims that were previously available and simply channel them from the overburdened courts to the original sentencing courts.[26] Justice Jackson's dissent further disputed the idea that Jones should have been barred from bringing a successive § 2255 motion in the first place.[27] She wrote that not only is there no evidence that Congress ever considered legal innocence claims when drafting the two exceptions to the bar on successive petitions, but, in fact, this type of claim was inadvertently omitted.[28]

Justice Jackson concluded her dissent by sharply disagreeing with the Court's approach to habeas corpus in this and other cases.[29] She wrote, "All of these opinions have now collectively managed to transform a statute that Congress designed to provide for a rational and orderly process of federal postconviction judicial review into an aimless and chaotic exercise in futility. The route to obtaining collateral relief is presently replete with imagined artificial barriers, arbitrary dead ends, and traps for the unwary. And today's turn makes the journey palpably absurd."[30]

Samia v. United States: Confrontation Clause

Adam Samia, Joseph Hunter, and Carl Stillwell were jointly prosecuted in federal court for the murder-for-hire of Catherine Lee, a real estate broker.[31] The government contended that Hunter had hired Samia and Stillwell to pose as buyers and visit properties with Lee.[32] When they were in a van together, the government maintained that Samia shot Lee.[33]

After his arrest, Stillwell confessed to being in the van when Samia shot Lee.[34] Stillwell did not testify at trial.[35] The prosecution sought to introduce this statement through an agent of the Drug Enforcement Agency (DEA).[36] The agent testified that Stillwell had confessed to "a time when the other person he was with pulled the trigger on that woman in a van that he and Mr. Stillwell was driving" but never mentioned Samia's name.[37] Throughout the agent's testimony, the agent only referred to the "other person."[38]

Both before the agent's testimony and again before deliberations, the District Court instructed the jury that the agent's testimony about Stillwell's confession was admissible only as to Stillwell and should not be considered as to Samia or Hunter.[39]

Samia and his codefendants were convicted on all counts.[40] Samia argued that his rights under the Confrontation Clause were violated by allowing the jury to hear Stillwell's confession that implicated Samia.[41]

The Supreme Court, in a 6–3 decision, split along ideological lines, found no violation of the Confrontation Clause.[42] Justice Thomas wrote the opinion for the majority. He began by recognizing that the Confrontation Clause applies because the statements from Stillwell were "testimonial."[43]

But the Court said that "the Confrontation Clause applies only to witnesses "against the accused. And [o]rdinarily, a witness whose testimony is introduced at a joint trial is not considered to be a witness 'against' a defendant if the jury is instructed to consider that testimony only against a codefendant. This general rule is consistent with the text of the Clause, historical practice, and the law's reliance on limiting instructions in other contexts."[44]

The Court distinguished *Bruton v. United States*, which the Court said "'recognized a narrow exception to' the presumption that juries follow their instructions, holding 'that a defendant is deprived of his Sixth Amendment right of confrontation when the facially incriminating confession of a nontestifying codefendant is introduced at their joint trial,' even with a proper instruction."[45] The Court said that there is a basic difference "between confessions that directly implicate a defendant and those that do so indirectly. Under these precedents, and consistent with the longstanding historical practice discussed above, the introduction here of Stillwell's altered confession coupled with a limiting instruction did not violate the Confrontation Clause."[46]

The Court rejected what it saw as expanding *Bruton*. The Court said it would be impractical and effectively require severance whenever the prosecution wishes to introduce the confession of a nontestifying codefendant in a joint trial. Justice Thomas concluded the majority opinion: "The Confrontation Clause ensures that defendants have the opportunity to confront witnesses against them, but it does not provide a freestanding guarantee against the risk of potential prejudice that may arise inferentially in a joint trial. Here, the Clause was not violated by the admission of a nontestifying codefendant's confession that did not directly inculpate the defendant and was subject to a proper limiting instruction."[47]

Justice Kagan wrote a strong dissent, joined by Justices Sotomayor and Jackson. She said that the Court drew an arbitrary distinction from *Bruton* that effectively undermines that decision. She concluded: "But contrary to today's decision, the serious Sixth Amendment problem remains. Now, defendants in joint trials will not have the chance to confront some of the most damaging witnesses against them. And a constitutional right once guaranteeing that opportunity will no longer. It will become, in joint trials, a shell of its former self."[48]

Justice Jackson also wrote a dissent in which she stressed that the majority began with a presumption in favor of allowing Stillwell's statement to be heard by the jury, rather than starting with the recognition of a serious Confrontation Clause problem. She said, "Under the majority's approach, the default rule is that a nontestifying codefendant's incriminating confession is admissible, so long as it is accompanied by a limiting instruction. Thus, for present purposes, the majority repeatedly calls, a 'narrow exception"' to this default rule. . . . That approach inverts the constitutional principles that govern this case. Under our well-established Sixth Amendment precedents, the Court's analysis must, instead, start from the premise that the introduction of Stillwell's inculpatory confession during the joint trial threatened Samia's Confrontation Clause rights."[49]

The dissenting justices saw this as a major change in the Confrontation Clause and a significant limit on the application of *Bruton* in situations when one defendant's statement is read without the opportunity for cross-examination, and it implicates a co-defendant.[50]

Reed v. Goertz: Statute of Limitations for Seeking DNA Evidence

In *Reed v. Goertz*, the Court resolved a Circuit split over when the statute of limitations for a 42 U.S.C. § 1983 claim seeking DNA testing of crime-scene evidence begins to run.[51] The Fifth Circuit had held that the statute of limitations began to run when the state *trial* court denied DNA testing, while the Eleventh Circuit held that it did not begin to run until the end of the entire state-court litigation had run its course, including appeals.[52] In a 6–3 decision, Justice Kavanaugh wrote for the majority ruling in favor of Reed that the statute of limitations begins when the entire litigation ends.[53]

In 1996, the State of Texas charged Rodney Reed with the murder of Stacey Stiles, and he was sentenced to death.[54] Reed asserted his innocence and, after his appeals and habeas petitions were unsuccessful, filed a motion in state court under Texas's postconviction DNA testing law to identify the real perpetrator.[55] But the state court in 2014 denied the motion because many of the items he requested to be tested were not preserved through an adequate chain of custody, and Reed did not show that he would have been acquitted if the DNA results were exculpatory.[56] The Texas Court of Criminal Appeals affirmed the denial in April 2017 and declined to reconsider in October 2017.[57]

In 2019, Reed filed a federal civil rights lawsuit against the local district attorney arguing that Texas's postconviction DNA testing law failed to provide him with procedural due process by requiring him to comply with various unconstitutional procedures to obtain DNA testing.[58] For example, the law required Reed to demonstrate that the evidence met the chain-of-custody requirement and was not contaminated. This is functionally impossible for inmates, however, as law enforcement has control over the evidence and may contaminate important pieces of evidence by storing them in the same box. The district court dismissed Reed's suit, and the Fifth Circuit affirmed, reasoning that Reed had brought the lawsuit too late.[59] The Fifth Circuit found that the two-year statute of limitations in Texas's postconviction DNA testing law began to run after the 2014 denial of testing and was thus long expired when Reed filed his federal case in 2019.[60]

Texas advanced three arguments: that Reed lacked standing, that the state has sovereign immunity, and that the procedural due process claim contravenes the *Rooker-Feldman* doctrine, which precludes lower federal courts from reviewing state court decisions. Justice Kavanaugh, joined by all except for Justices Alito and Gorsuch, rejected each of these arguments. First, the Court said that Reed suffered an injury when the state prosecutor denied him access to the evidence, which the court could remedy by finding that the testing procedures violated due process.[61] Second, Texas cannot invoke the state's sovereign immunity because the *Ex parte Young* doctrine allows suits for declaratory or injunctive relief against state officers working in their official capacities.[62] Finally, the *Rooker-Feldman* doctrine prevents federal courts from considering cases brought when a losing party in a state-court case challenges that judgment. But here, Reed is challenging the procedures in the Texas statute, not the unfavorable ruling itself.[63]

The Court's decision that the statute of limitations should begin after the conclusion of the entire state litigation process is based on the idea that the plaintiff must have a "complete and present cause of action," which the Court determines by focusing on the specific constitutional right alleged to have been infringed.[64] Here, the right in question is Reed's liberty interest in DNA testing. Because this right hinges on the state process for considering the request, the failure to provide the fair process could not be complete until Texas was done considering the request.[65] Therefore, the Court found that the statute of limitations could not begin to run until the Texas Court of Criminal Appeals denied Reed's motion for rehearing in October 2017.[66]

The majority further justified the decision by emphasizing the consequences of the alternative approach.[67] It would be inefficient for a plaintiff to file a federal claim while the state appeals process was still ongoing.[68] Further, the system would confuse litigants who expect the courthouse doors to be open yet find that they closed long ago.

Justices Alito, joined by Gorsuch in dissent, disagreed with the majority's judgment as to when the statute of limitations should begin to run.[69] He did not find it unfair to require plaintiffs to sue within two years of the state high court decision—writing that "one need not have 'supernatural foresight' in order to predict that rehearing is unlikely to be granted."[70]

Cruz v. Arizona: Supreme Court Review of State Court Decisions

In one of the first decisions of the 2022–2023 term, the Supreme Court delivered a rare victory for people on death row by clarifying when federal courts may intervene when a state court fails to apply federal law.

In 2005, John Montenegro Cruz was convicted of first-degree capital murder for killing a police officer.[71] Arizona law rendered him ineligible for parole based on the capital charge. Therefore, the only sentencing options available were life imprisonment without parole or the death penalty. Cruz's lawyer repeatedly tried to inform the jury that a life sentence meant no possibility of parole, but the trial judge denied his request.[72] Instead, the trial judge incorrectly informed the jury that if they did not select a death sentence, the judge could choose *either* life without parole or the possibility of parole after 25 years.[73] This detail was significant, as a previous Supreme Court ruling in *Simmons v. South Carolina* established the right of capital defendants to inform the jury when it was a life sentence with no possibility of parole.[74] *Simmons* hinged on the idea that a defendant is entitled to a jury fully informed of parole ineligibility when "future dangerousness is at issue" in the sentencing decision.[75] Cruz argued before the Arizona trial court and supreme court that his due process rights were violated, but both courts found that *Simmons* did not apply in Arizona.[76]

After Cruz's trial and appeal concluded, the Supreme Court held in *Lynch v.* Arizona that *Simmons* unequivocally applied in Arizona.[77] Thus, Cruz raised the issue again in a state postconviction petition.[78] Arizona Rule of Criminal Procedure 32.1(g) allows defendants to file successive petitions if there has been a significant change of law that would "probably overturn the defendant's judgment or sentence."[79] The Arizona Supreme Court found that *Lynch* was not a significant change because it merely changed the *application* of the law, not the law itself given that *Simmons* was already established law.[80]

The Supreme Court, in a 5–4 decision, reversed the Arizona courts. Justice Sotomayor wrote for the Court, joined by Chief Justice Roberts and Justices Kagan, Kavanaugh, and Jackson. The key question the Court answered was procedural: Is the Arizona Supreme Court's ruling that a state rule of criminal procedure precluded postconviction relief an "adequate" state law ground for the judgment against him, thereby precluding review by the Supreme Court?[81] The law is clear that the United States Supreme Court cannot review a state court decision that is based on an independent and adequate state law ground.[82]

Arizona argued that the application of Rule 32.1(g) was such an independent and adequate state law ground precluding Supreme Court jurisdiction. The Court rejected this argument. But the Court found this to be one of the "rarest of situations" where the state decision was "so unfounded as to be essentially arbitrary," rendering the state grounds "inadequate to stop consideration of a federal question."[83]

The Court reasoned that the Arizona Supreme Court had been squarely in the wrong by not considering *Lynch* to be transformative. Arizona refused to apply *Simmons* for over two decades, so it is "harder to imagine a clearer break from the past" than *Lynch* overruling binding Arizona precedent.[84] Further, the state had never before found overturning of a binding precedent to fail Rule 32.1(g).[85]

Justice Barrett, joined by Thomas, Alito, and Gorsuch, wrote a dissent emphasizing the importance of federalism and deference to state courts on issues of state law. The dissent argued that Arizona was right to deem *Lynch* nontransformative, though the majority clarifies this point writing that "[w]hile *Lynch* did not change this Court's interpretation of *Simmons*, it did change the operative (and mistaken) interpretation of *Simmons* by Arizona."[86]

Although Cruz's conviction is not directly impacted, the decision still has important consequences for the defendant as he will be entitled to a new sentencing hearing. Cruz, along with 30 others in the same position in Arizona, will now go before a jury that knows that if they grant a life sentence, they will never receive parole. This is particularly significant in Cruz's case, as multiple jurors from his original trial expressed a desire to vote for life without the possibility of parole. The case also clarifies situations where state court decisions based on state law do not constitute independent and adequate state law grounds precluding Supreme Court review.

Endnotes

1. 143 S. Ct. 1857 (2023).
2. *Id.* at 1863–64.
3. *Id.* at 1864.
4. *Id.*
5. *Id.* at 1891 (Jackson, J., dissenting).
6. *Id.* at 1864.
7. *Id.* at 1879 (Jackson, J., dissenting).
8. *Id.*
9. *Id.*
10. *Id.* at 1866.
11. *Id.* at 1867.
12. *Id.*
13. *Id.* at 1864.
14. *Id.*
15. *Id.* at 1864, 1867.
16. *Id.* at 1864.
17. *Id.*
18. *Id.* at 1868.
19. *Id.*
20. *Id.* at 1866.
21. *Id.* at 1869.
22. *Id.*
23. *Id.* at 1877 (Sotomayor, J., dissenting).
24. *Id.* at 1878 (Jackson, J., dissenting).
25. *Id.* at 1879–82.
26. *Id.* at 1881–82.
27. *Id.* at 1885–86.
28. *Id.* at 1885.
29. *Id.* at 1898.
30. *Id.*
31. Samia v. United States, 143 S. Ct. 2004, 2010 (2023).
32. *Id.* at 2011.
33. *Id.*
34. *Id.* at 2010.
35. *Id.*
36. *Id.*
37. *Id.* at 2011.
38. *Id.*
39. *Id.*

40. *Id.*
41. *Id.* at 2011–12.
42. *Id.* at 2014.
43. *Id.* at 2012.
44. *Id.*
45. *Id.* at 2014.
46. *Id.*
47. *Id.* at 2018.
48. *Id.* at 2025.
49. *Id.* at 2025–26.
50. *Id.* at 2021–22.
51. *Reed v. Goertz*, 143 S. Ct. 955, 962 (2023).
52. *Id.* at 959.
53. *Id.*
54. *Id.*
55. *Id.*
56. *Id.* at 960.
57. *Id.*
58. *Id.*
59. *Id.*
60. *Id.*
61. *Id.*
62. *Id.*
63. *Id.*
64. *Id.*
65. *Id.* at 961.
66. *Id.*
67. *Id.*
68. *Id.*
69. *Id.* at 973–77.
70. *Id.* at 977.
71. *Cruz v. Ariz.*, 143 S. Ct. 650, 654 (2023).
72. *Id.* at 656.
73. *Id.*
74. *Simmons v. South Carolina*, 512 U.S. 154, 162 (1994).
75. *Id.* at 161.
76. *Cruz v. Ariz*, 143 S. Ct. 650 at 655 (2023).
77. *Id.* at 656.
78. *Id.*
79. *Id.* at 657.
80. *Id.* at 658.

81. *Id.* at 658.
82. *See* ERWIN CHEMERINSKY, FEDERAL JURISDICTION ch. 10 (8th ed. 2021).
83. *Cruz v. Ariz*, 143 S. Ct. 650 at 658 (2023).
84. *Id.* at 659.
85. *Id.* at 665.
86. *Id.* at 660.

5

Dormant Commerce Clause

National Pork Producers v. Ross was a major ruling upholding the authority of state and local governments to regulate the sale and production of products within their borders.[1] The Court, albeit in a very fragmented decision, upheld the constitutionality of a California law that required that pork sold in the state come from humanely treated pigs.[2] In doing so, the Court affirmed state and local government's ability to regulate what is sold within their borders, even if it limits goods and services from other states.[3]

What Is the Dormant Commerce Clause?

The *dormant commerce clause* is the principle that state and local laws are unconstitutional if they place an undue burden on interstate commerce. No constitutional provision expressly declares that states may not burden interstate commerce; rather, the Supreme Court has inferred this principle from the grant of power to Congress in Article I, § 8 to regulate commerce among the states.[4] A major impetus for the Constitutional Convention in 1787 was how state governments were creating trade barriers among themselves. States with ports charged high fees for landlocked states to have access, and then those states retaliated. The dormant commerce clause is founded on the premise that free trade among the states is essential, and every grower or manufacturer should have access to all markets.

When considering the relationship between federal and state or local laws, if Congress has legislated, the question is whether federal law preempts state or local law. Even if Congress has not acted or no preemption is found, the state or local law can be challenged on the ground that it excessively burdens commerce among the states. In other words, even if Congress has not legislated—even if its commerce power lies dormant—state and local laws can still be challenged as unduly impeding interstate commerce. Justice Felix Frankfurter explained, "[T]he doctrine [is] that the commerce clause, by its own force and without national legislation, puts it into the power of the Court to place limits on state authority."[5]

Facts

National Pork Producers involved a California initiative, Proposition 12, that forbids the sale of whole pork meat in the state from breeding pigs (or their immediate offspring) that are "confined in a cruel manner."[6] Confinement is "cruel" if it prevents a pig from "lying down, standing up, fully extending [its] limbs, or turning around freely."[7]

The National Pork Producers Council and the American Farm Bureau Federation filed a lawsuit on behalf of those who raise and process pigs.[8] Under the commerce clause, they alleged that Proposition 12 violates the Constitution by impermissibly burdening interstate commerce.[9] Most pork sold in California is produced out of state, much of it in Iowa.[10]

The plaintiffs claimed that California acted unconstitutionally in regulating activity outside its borders.[11] They said that the dormant commerce clause should preclude states from imposing regulations on how business is done in other states.[12] California, in response, argued that it was regulating just what was sold in that state, and it is a state's prerogative to regulate what is bought and sold within its borders.[13]

If the Supreme Court had accepted the plaintiff's argument, the implications would be enormous because state laws frequently have a disproportionate effect on out-of-staters. California could not set stricter emissions standards for vehicles because most are manufactured out of the state. A recently adopted New York law preventing the use of natural gas in new construction to shift from fossil fuels would not be allowed because natural gas is almost entirely produced in other states. A state could not prevent the use of particular pesticides if they were manufactured elsewhere. The examples are endless. Adopting the pork producers' argument would greatly weaken states' ability to protect their residents.

The Court's Decision

The Supreme Court, in a 5–4 decision, rejected the challenge to the California initiative and followed well-established principles.[14] Although the justices agreed to the basic analytical framework regarding the dormant commerce clause, there was significant disagreement about its application when a state or local law is not discriminatory.[15] Indeed, there was no majority opinion of the Court.

Justice Gorsuch announced the judgment for the Court and reaffirmed, for a majority of the justices, that a state or local law is presumed unconstitutional if it treats in-staters and out-of-staters differently.[16] The Court stated: "Today, this antidiscrimination principle lies at the 'very core' of our dormant Commerce Clause jurisprudence. In its 'modern' cases, this Court has said that the Commerce Clause prohibits the enforcement of state laws 'driven by . . . 'economic protectionism—that is, regulatory measures designed to benefit in-state economic interests by burdening out-of-state competitors.'"[17]

All justices agreed with this interpretation: if a state or local law burdens interstate commerce and discriminates against out-of-staters, there is a strong presumption that it violates the dormant commerce clause. But the disagreement was over how to treat a nondiscriminatory law that burdens interstate commerce.

California's Proposition 12 is not discriminatory because it applies the same standards for pork sold in the state to both in-state and out-of-state companies.[18] In fact, the challengers did not claim that the California law was discriminatory or protectionist legislation.[19] As Justice Gorsuch noted: "[The challengers] do not allege that California's law seeks to advantage in-state firms or disadvantage out-of-state rivals. In fact, petitioners *disavow* any discrimination-based claim, conceding that Proposition 12 imposes the same burdens on in-state pork producers that it imposes on out-of-state ones."[20]

If a state law is not discriminatory, the Supreme Court has long maintained that it should be upheld unless it excessively burdens interstate commerce in relation to its benefits. The Court articulated this in *Pike v. Bruce Church, Inc.*, with Justice Stewart writing, "Where the statute regulates even-handedly to effectuate a legitimate local public interest, and its effects on interstate commerce are only incidental, it will be upheld unless the burden imposed on such commerce is clearly excessive in relation to the putative local benefits."[21]

The justices disagreed as to the application of this test. Justice Gorsuch, joined by Justice Thomas, objected to using the balancing test when there is no discrimination against out-of-staters.[22] He argued that this inevitably leads to arbitrary decisions because courts balance incommensurate interests.[23] Justice Gorsuch wrote, "So even accepting everything petitioners say, we remain left with a task no court is equipped to undertake. On the one hand, some out-of-state producers who choose to comply with Proposition 12 may incur new costs. On the other hand, the law serves moral and health interests of some (disputable) magnitude for in-state residents. Some might reasonably find one set of concerns more compelling. Others might fairly disagree. How should we settle that dispute? The competing goods are incommensurable. Your guess is as good as ours. More accurately, your guess is *better* than ours. In a functioning democracy, policy choices like these usually belong to the people and their elected representatives."[24]

Justice Gorsuch stressed that if pork producers don't like California's regulation, they can persuade Congress to use its commerce clause power to preempt such laws. He explained, "While the Constitution addresses many weighty issues, the type of pork chops California merchants may sell is not on that list."[25]

Justice Sotomayor, joined by Justice Kagan, concurred. Unlike Justice Gorsuch, she did not want to change the law when a state or local law is not discriminatory and instead wanted to apply the well-established *Pike* balancing test. She wrote, "I vote to affirm the judgment because petitioners fail to allege a substantial burden on interstate commerce as required by *Pike*, not because of any fundamental reworking of that doctrine."[26] Justice Sotomayor said that the initial requirement under the dormant commerce clause always is that there be a burden on interstate commerce, and the plaintiffs had not alleged that here.[27] She wrote: "Alleging a substantial burden on interstate commerce is a threshold requirement that plaintiffs must satisfy before courts need even engage in *Pike*'s balancing and tailoring analyses. Because petitioners have not done so, they fail to state a *Pike* claim."[28]

Justice Barrett wrote a concurring opinion in which she agreed with Justice Gorsuch.[29] She explained that balancing is possible only when commensurate things are being weighed, and here, there was no way for a court to do the balancing.[30] She said that she wrote separately to stress that unlike Justices Sotomayor and Kagan, she saw the California law as placing a substantial burden on interstate commerce.[31] She wrote: "I disagree with my colleagues who would hold that petitioners have failed to allege a substantial burden on interstate commerce. The complaint plausibly alleges that Proposition 12's costs are pervasive, burdensome, and will be felt primarily (but not exclusively) outside California. If the burdens and benefits were capable of judicial balancing, I would permit petitioners to proceed with their *Pike* claim."[32] That means for Justice Barrett, *Pike* balancing occurs only when there are comparable things to balance. This interpretation would greatly restrict the application of the dormant commerce clause when state and local laws are not discriminatory. It appears then that there are three justices—Gorsuch, Thomas, and Barrett—who would not apply the dormant commerce clause in instances where the state or local government is not discriminating against out-of-staters.

Chief Justice Roberts concurred in part and dissented in part, joined by Justices Alito, Kavanaugh, and Jackson.[33] He stressed that this case was on a motion to dismiss and that the complaint alleged significant economic harms from the California law. He concluded: "In my view, petitioners plausibly allege a substantial burden against interstate commerce. I would therefore remand the case for the Ninth Circuit to decide whether it is plausible that the "burden . . . is clearly excessive in relation to the putative local benefits.'"[34]

Justice Kavanaugh wrote a concurring opinion saying that he agreed with Chief Justice Roberts, but that there might be other ways of successfully challenging the California law. He stated, "I add this opinion to point out that state economic regulations like California's Proposition 12 may raise questions not only under the Commerce Clause, but also under the Import-Export Clause, the Privileges and Immunities Clause, and the Full Faith and Credit Clause."[35]

What Does It Mean?

The Court emphatically rejected the Pork Producers' claim that a law is unconstitutional simply because its effect is regulating those out of state.[36] There was strong consensus among the justices that the dormant commerce clause focuses on state and local laws that discriminate against out-of-state goods and services.[37] Such protectionist legislation rarely survives dormant commerce clause analysis. Six justices "affirmatively retain the longstanding *Pike* balancing test for analyzing dormant Commerce Clause challenges to state economic regulations."[38] And five justices vote to uphold the California law but for very different reasons.[39] Yet it obviously also is clear that this a Court that is very divided over the dormant commerce clause, especially when a state or local law is not discriminatory.

Ultimately, the Supreme Court held that California gets to decide what is sold in California so long as it treats in-state producers and out-of-state producers alike. Under the Constitution, Congress, using its power to regulate commerce among the states, could override this and decree national standards for pork production or other areas of business. But unless and until Congress does this, states should be able to decide for themselves.

In one sense, the decision is unremarkable because it follows decades of precedents. Its major significance is that it did not change the law. The decision did not impose new and significant restrictions on the ability of states to regulate, whether to protect the environment or, as here, to enhance humane treatment of animals.

Yet, in another way the decision is remarkable because the Roberts Court historically has been so protective of business in rulings across areas of law. In this context, upholding the California law is notable and crucial. It gives states great latitude to regulate what is sold in its borders, even when there is a disproportionate effect on out-of-staters.

Endnotes

1. 143 S. Ct. 1142, 1150 (2023).
2. *Id.* at 1150–51.
3. *Id.* The dormant commerce clause also arose in another case this term. In *Mallory v. Norfolk Railway*, 143 S. Ct. 2028 (2023), Justice Alito's concurring opinion focused on the dormant commerce clause as a limit on the ability of a state to require that out-of-state businesses to register and consent to personal jurisdiction. *Mallory* is discussed in Chapter 14.
4. U.S. Const. art. I § 8 cl. 3 ("Congress shall have Power . . . to regulate commerce . . . *among the several states*." (emphasis added)).
5. Felix Frankfurter, The Commerce Clause Under Marshall, Taney & Waite 18 (1937).
6. 143 S. Ct. 1142, 1150 (2023).
7. *Id.* at 1150–51.
8. *Id.* at 1151.
9. *Id.*
10. *Id.* at 1173.
11. *Id.* at 1153–55.
12. *Id.* at 1154–55.
13. *Id.* at 1150–51.
14. *Id.* at 1150, 1153–65.
15. *Id.* at 1153–76.
16. *Id.* at 1152.
17. *Id.* at 1153.
18. *Id.*
19. *Id.*
20. *Id.* at 1153.
21. 397 U.S. 137, 142 (1970).
22. 143 S. Ct. at 1159–60.
23. *Id.* at 1160.
24. *Id.*

25. *Id.* at 1149.
26. *Id.* at 1165 (Sotomayor, J., concurring).
27. *Id.*at 1165–66.
28. *Id.* at 1166.
29. *Id.* at 1166–67 (Barrett, J., concurring).
30. *Id.* at 1167.
31. *Id.*
32. *Id.*
33. *Id.* at 1167–72 (Roberts, C.J., concurring in part and dissenting in part).
34. *Id.* at 1169–72.
35. *Id.* at 1172 (Kavanaugh, J., concurring).
36. *Id.* at 1151–52.
37. *Id.* at 1152–53.
38. *Id.* at 1172.
39. *Id.* at 1165–76.

6

Election Law

After a decade of weakening protections for voting rights, the Supreme Court this term handed down important victories protecting the electoral process. These rulings must be understood in the context of the Supreme Court's recent record on voting. In 2013, in *Shelby County v. Holder*, the Supreme Court declared unconstitutional crucial provisions of the Voting Rights Act that required state and local governments with a history of race discrimination in voting to get pre-approval of significant changes in their election systems.[1] In 2019, in *Rucho v. Common Cause*, the Court held that federal courts can never hear challenges to partisan gerrymandering.[2] In 2021, in *Brnovich v. Democratic National Committee*, the Court interpreted the Voting Rights Act to make it much more difficult to prove that state and local election practices, such as restrictions on absentee ballots, are racially discriminatory.[3]

These cases led some to have concerns when the Court took two election cases to decide during October Term 2022. But contrary to the predictions and expectations of many, the Supreme Court ruled in favor of voting rights in both cases. One involved the Voting Rights Act, and the other concerned a state court's ability to enforce a state's constitution on congressional elections.

Allen v. Milligan[4]

Section 2 of the Voting Rights Act prevents state and local governments from having election systems that discriminate against voters of color.[5] In 1982, Congress amended this to make clear that the law prohibits laws that have a discriminatory effect against minority voters; there does not have to be proof that the government had a racially discriminatory purpose.[6]

But, as mentioned above, two years ago, in *Brnovich v. Democratic National Committee*, the Court made it much harder to use § 2 to challenge state and local election laws that regulate voting—such as rules on absentee ballots and the location of polling places.[7] In an ideologically split decision, the Court not only made it difficult to prove race discrimination but also said that there must be consideration of the state's interest in preventing voter fraud, something never mentioned in the Voting Rights Act.[8]

Against this backdrop, the Court's decision in *Allen v. Milligan* is most significant for what the Court didn't do: It did not further weaken the law of voting rights as many expected. The case involved another key application of § 2 of the Voting Rights Act: when the drawing of election districts is impermissibly racially discriminatory.

The case arose in Alabama. That state's population is about 27 percent Black individuals. Alabama has seven seats in the House of Representatives. After the 2020 census, the Alabama legislature engaged in redistricting and packed Black voters in one of the seven districts and spread them around the others, with the effect that Alabama was very likely to have only one Black representative in Congress.[9] The outcome was that there likely would be six, not five, Republicans elected to Congress from Alabama.

The Supreme Court, following decades-old precedents, found that this violated the Voting Rights Act. The decision was 5–4, with Chief Justice Roberts writing a majority opinion joined by Justices Sotomayor, Kagan, Kavanaugh, and Jackson.

In *Thornburgh v. Gingles*, the Court articulated a three-part test for determining when election districting is racially discriminatory.[10] The Supreme Court summarized these requirements: "To succeed in proving a § 2 violation under *Gingles*, plaintiffs must satisfy three 'preconditions.' First, the 'minority group must be sufficiently large and [geographically] compact to constitute a majority in a reasonably configured district.' A district will be reasonably configured, our cases explain, if it comports with traditional districting criteria, such as being contiguous and reasonably compact. Second, the minority group must be able to show that it is politically cohesive.' And third, 'the minority must be able to demonstrate that the white majority votes sufficiently as a bloc to enable it . . . to defeat the minority's preferred candidate.' Finally, a plaintiff who demonstrates the three preconditions must also show, under the 'totality of circumstances,' that the political process is not 'equally open' to minority voters."[11]

The Court affirmed a three-judge federal district court's conclusion that these requirements were met. The Court relied on the factfinding by the district court.[12] Adopting the district court's conclusion, the Court agreed that record "'strongly suggest[ed] that Black voters in Alabama' could constitute a majority in a second, reasonably configured, district."[13] The Court quoted the district court's conclusion that there was "no serious dispute that Black voters are politically cohesive, nor that the challenged districts' white majority votes sufficiently as a bloc to usually defeat Black voters' preferred candidate."[14]

Many, including me, predicted that the Court would use *Allen v. Milligan* to weaken or overrule this test. But contrary to these predictions, Chief Justice Roberts' opinion for the Court applied the *Thornburgh v. Gingles* test and found that Alabama violated the Voting Rights Act.

Alabama argued to the Court that those who draw maps should be unable to look at race and that equal protection requires that they be color-blind.[15] This would mean that there cannot be liability based on racially disparate impact and would effectively nullify the 1982 amendments to the Voting Rights Act. The Supreme Court expressly rejected that view, declaring: "The contention that mapmakers must be entirely 'blind' to race has no footing in our § 2 case law."[16] Indeed, the Supreme Court expressly rejected Alabama's contention that the Voting Rights Act is unconstitutional in creating disparate impact liability.

Justice Kavanaugh wrote a concurring opinion.[17] He stressed *stare decisis* in the Court not overruling *Thornburgh v. Gingles*: "[T]he upshot of Alabama's argument is that the Court should overrule *Gingles*. But the *stare decisis* standard for this Court to overrule a statutory precedent, as distinct from a constitutional precedent, is comparatively strict. Unlike with constitutional precedents, Congress and the President may enact new legislation to alter statutory precedents such as *Gingles*."[18] Like Chief Justice Roberts, he stressed that the Voting Rights Act does not require proportional representation but allows liability based on a racially disparate impact.[19] But Justice Kavanaugh did raise the possibility that discrimination in voting has sufficiently lessened to make the *Thornburgh* test unnecessary.

The dissents were strenuous and would have dramatically changed the law on the Voting Rights Act. Justice Thomas began his dissent by saying, "These cases 'are yet another installment in the 'disastrous misadventure' of this Court's voting rights jurisprudence.'"[20] He objected to liability based on disparate impact and said that was inconsistent with a constitutional requirement for color blindness. He wrote: "The question presented is whether § 2 of the Act, as amended, requires the State of Alabama to intentionally redraw its longstanding congressional districts so that black voters can control a number of seats roughly proportional to the black share of the State's population. Section 2 demands no such thing, and, if it did, the Constitution would not permit it."[21] He would have ruled that the Voting Rights Act can never be used for claims of discrimination in the drawing of single member election districts.[22]

Justice Alito would have barred the use of race in deciding whether an election district violated the Act. He would keep but recast the *Thornbugh v. Gingles* test in a way that would make it much harder to prove a violation of Section 2 of the Voting Rights Act.[23]

Either of the dissenters' approach would further gut this important civil rights statute. But the majority opinion by Chief Justice Roberts forcefully rejects these arguments, reaffirms precedents, and holds that Voting Rights Act can continue to be used to challenge race discrimination in drawing election districts based on discriminatory effects. Soon after the Court decided this case, it found that Louisiana had likewise violated the Voting Rights Act in its drawing of election districts.[24]

Moore v. Harper

The stakes in *Moore v. Harper* were enormous.[25] The case arose in North Carolina and involved whether state courts can enforce state constitutional requirements on elections.

North Carolina is a purple state, closely divided between Democrats and Republicans. Barack Obama carried the state in 2008, but Mitt Romney won in 2012, and Donald Trump prevailed in the last two presidential elections. But it was always by a close margin. Trump beat Biden by 1.35 percent.

After the 2020 Census, North Carolina gained an additional member of Congress; because of its population growth, apportionment entitled it to 14 congressional seats.[26] Like all states, North Carolina redrew the election districts. The legislature drew the congressional districts so that Republicans would likely win 10 of the 14 races.[27] The North Carolina Supreme Court held that this violated the North Carolina constitution and appointed a commission to redraw the districts.[28] Nonpartisan districts were used in November 2022, with both Republicans and Democrats winning seven seats, which is to be expected in an election when the parties statewide received almost the same number of votes.

The leaders of the North Carolina legislature and its supporters went to the United States Supreme Court to contend that the North Carolina Supreme Court has no legal authority to be involved, that the state legislature gets the last, unreviewable word.[29] They based this argument on a provision of Article I, § 4 of the Constitution, which says that the legislature of each state must determine the "time, place, and manner" for choosing its members in Congress.[30] This is called the "independent state legislature theory." Chief Justice William Rehnquist first suggested it in a concurring opinion in *Bush v. Gore* in 2000. The theory provides that the legislature gets the only and final say; state courts are powerless to enforce their laws.[31]

The implications of the independent state legislature theory are enormous. It would mean that no court, state or federal, could hear challenges to partisan gerrymandering for congressional seats, no matter how egregious. Also, it would mean that independent districting commissions, such as exist in California and several other states, would be unconstitutional for House of Representative elections. Finally, and most damaging, it could mean that state legislatures could ignore the popular vote in allocating electors in presidential elections, and state courts would be powerless to enforce state laws requiring that the winner of the popular vote get the states' electors in the Electoral College. There is another provision of the Constitution, in Article II, § 1, that says that the legislatures of each state will allocate the electors from that state to the Electoral College.[32] This was the basis for Donald Trump trying unsuccessfully to persuade Republican legislatures in Wisconsin, Michigan, Pennsylvania, and Georgia to give him their electoral votes, notwithstanding Biden winning the popular vote in those states.

The Court in *Moore v. Harper* emphatically rejected the independent state legislature theory. Chief Justice Roberts wrote for the Court in a 6–3 decision and held that state courts have the power to enforce state law, including with regard to elections.[33] A procedural wrinkle emerged that raises the question of whether the Court should have even decided the case. The results of the November 2022 election changed the political composition of North Carolina's Supreme Court. It went from a 4–3 Democratic majority to a 5–2 Republican one. In 2023, the newly constituted North Carolina Supreme Court reversed the decision that had found the districting to violate the state constitution.[34]

The Supreme Court asked for a briefing about the significance of the reconsideration by the North Carolina Supreme Court.[35] Chief Justice Roberts, writing for the Court, said that the North Carolina Supreme Court decision was a final judgment and thus reviewable by the United States Supreme Court.[36] The Court said that if it reversed the North Carolina Supreme Court the 2021 congressional maps would go into effect, which was enough to make the case justiciable.[37] Justice Thomas, in a dissent, strongly disagreed. He said the case was moot because the lower court decision had been reversed, and the maps used in the 2022 election never would be used.[38]

My sense is that Justice Thomas makes a strong argument for mootness. But the majority wanted to resolve this issue before the next presidential election rather than risking the need to decide it in the context of deciding who will be the next president.

Reaching the merits, Chief Justice Roberts held that state courts have the authority to enforce state constitutions. He invoked *Marbury v. Madison*, the 1803 decision that famously recognized the power of courts to review the constitutionality of executive and legislative actions.[39] He said that the power of judicial review in the states precedes *Marbury* and that the Election Clause of the Constitution does not keep state courts from exercising judicial review and enforcing state constitutions.[40] He wrote: "The argument advanced by the defendants and the dissent also does not account for the Framers' understanding that when legislatures make laws, they are bound by the provisions of the very documents that give them life. Legislatures, the Framers recognized, 'are the mere creatures of the State Constitutions, and cannot be greater than their creators.' *Marbury* confirmed this understanding, and nothing in the text of the Elections Clause undermines it."[41]

The Court was thus emphatic that the elections clause of Article I, § 4 does not keep state courts from reviewing the acts of state legislatures with regard to congressional elections. The Court declared: "We are asked to decide whether the Elections Clause carves out an exception to this basic principle. We hold that it does not. The Elections Clause does not insulate state legislatures from the ordinary exercise of state judicial review."[42]

The decision is thus an important victory for the power of state courts to ensure free and fair elections. But the last part of Chief Justice Roberts' opinion has caused concern among commentators.[43] He wrote, "Although we conclude that the Elections Clause does not exempt state legislatures from the ordinary constraints imposed by state law, state courts do not have free rein."[44] At the end of the opinion, he stated, "We hold only that state courts may not transgress the ordinary bounds of judicial review such that they arrogate to themselves the power vested in state legislatures to regulate federal elections."[45]

It is unclear what this means. What does Chief Justice Roberts consider the "ordinary bounds of judicial review"? What types of state court decisions would be going too far? In an opinion that forcefully rejected the independent state legislature theory, what was Chief Justice Roberts trying to say about when federal courts can get involved? Although he does not answer these questions and his statement is ambiguous, there is a way to read his language narrowly. In the same part of his opinion, Chief Justice Roberts wrote: "Running through each of these examples is the concern that state courts might read state law in such a manner as to circumvent federal constitutional provisions. Therefore, although mindful of the general rule of accepting state court interpretations of state law, we have tempered such deference when required by our duty to safeguard limits imposed by the Federal Constitution."[46] From this perspective, federal courts—including the Supreme Court—would be involved only if there was a claim that the state court violated the United States Constitution. No one, of course, would deny the Supreme Court a role in those circumstances. But there is ambiguity to Chief Justice Roberts' statement and concern about what it might mean in the future. It also is unclear how matters would come to federal court, other than to the Supreme Court, because federal district courts generally cannot review final decisions of state courts.

Justice Thomas, joined by Justices Alito and Gorsuch, dissented. He would have had the Court dismiss the case.[47] And if the Court reached the merits, he would likely have adopted the independent state legislature theory.[48]

Conclusion

These two decisions did not expand the protection for voting rights. But after a decade of the Supreme Court consistently restricting judicial protection of voting and elections, these cases are crucial for what they didn't do. They didn't change the law on when districting violates § 2 of the Voting Rights Act. They didn't adopt the independent state legislature theory. In this sense, they were important victories for voting rights.

Endnotes

1. 570 U.S. 529 (2013).
2. 139 S. Ct. 2484 (2019).
3. 141 S. Ct. 2321 (2021).
4. 143 S. Ct. 1487 (2023).
5. Voting Rights Act of 1965, 89 P.L. 110.
6. Voting Rights Act Amendments of 1982, 97 P.L. 205.
7. 141 U.S. at 2339–44.
8. *Id.* at 2340.
9. 143 U.S. at 1501.
10. 478 U.S. 30 (1986).

11. 143 S. Ct. 1487 at 1503.
12. *Id.* at 1504.
13. *Id.*
14. *Id.* at 1505.
15. *See id.* at 1506.
16. *Id.* at 1512.
17. *Id.* at 1517 (Kavanaugh, J., concurring).
18. *Id.*
19. *Id.* at 1518 (Kavanaugh, J., concurring).
20. *Id.* at 1519 (Thomas, J., dissenting).
21. *Id.*
22. *Id.* at 1544–45 (Thomas, J., dissenting).
23. *Id.* at 1548–49 (Alito, J., dissenting).
24. *Ardoin v. Robinson*, 2023 WL 4163160 (cert. denied).
25. 143 S. Ct. 2065 (2023).
26. U.S. Census Bureau, 2020 Census Apportionment Results (2021) (Table 1).
27. 143 S. Ct. 2065 at 2074.
28. *Id.*
29. *Id.* at 2075.
30. U.S. Const. art. I, §4, cl. 1.
31. *See Bush v. Gore*, 531 U.S. 98, 113–15 (2000) (Rehnquist, C.J., concurring) ("This inquiry does not imply a disrespect for state *courts* but rather a respect for the constitutionally prescribed role of state *legislatures*. To attach definitive weight to the pronouncement of a state court, when the very question at issue is whether the court has actually departed from the statutory meaning, would be to abdicate our responsibility to enforce the explicit requirements of Article II.").
32. U.S. Const. art. II, § 1, cl. 2 (Elector Appointments Clause).
33. 143 S. Ct. 2065 at 2079–88.
34. *Id.* at 2075.
35. *Id.*
36. *Id.* at 2079.
37. *Id.*
38. *Id.* at 2091–92 (Thomas, J., dissenting).
39. *See* 5 U.S. (1 Cranch) 137, 177 (1803).
40. 143 S. Ct. 2065 at 2080.
41. *Id.* at 2083–84 (internal citation and quotation removed).
42. *Id.* at 2081.
43. Richard H. Pildes, *The Supreme Court Rejected a Dangerous Elections Theory. But It's Not All Good News*, N.Y. Times (June 28, 2023), https://www.nytimes.com/2023/06/28/opinion/supreme-court-independent-state-legislature-theory.html; Richard L. Hasen, *There's a Time Bomb in Progressives' Big*

Supreme Court Voting Case Win, SLATE, (June 27, 2023, 12:44 PM), https://slate.com/news-and-politics/2023/06/supreme-court-voting-moore-v-harper-time-bomb.html.

44. 143 S. Ct. 2065 at 2088.
45. *Id.*
46. *Id.*
47. *Id.* at 2092.
48. *Id.* at 2105.

7

Environmental Law

The Supreme Court decided one major case concerning environmental law: *Sackett v. Environmental Protection Agency.*[1] This issue is when wetlands are considered "waters of the United States" under the Clean Water Act and therefore need to meet the requirements of that statute. The important environmental statute protects "the waters of the United States," but as Justice Alito asked, "[W]hat does that phrase mean? Does the term encompass any backyard that is soggy enough for some minimum period of time? Does it reach 'mudflats, sandflats, wetlands, sloughs, prairie potholes, wet meadows, [or] playa lakes'? How about ditches, swimming pools, and puddles?"[2] The case is thus significant in determining the scope and application of the Clean Water Act.

The Court held that the Clean Water Act extends only to wetlands that are "as a practical matter indistinguishable from waters of the United States."[3] The Court said that this requires the party seeking to apply the Clean Water Act must establish that the "adjacent body of water constitutes 'waters of the United States,'" and that "the wetland has a continuous surface connection with that water, making it difficult to determine where the 'water' ends and the 'wetland begins.'"[4] This restrictive interpretation of the Act will make it harder to apply to wetlands in the future. Although the justices were unanimous regarding the result, they split 5–4 on this narrow interpretation of the Clean Water Act.

Facts

Michael and Chantell Sackett purchased a lot near Priest Lake in Idaho in 2004 that they began backfilling with dirt and rocks in preparation for building a home on the property.[5] The Environmental Protection Agency (EPA) later sent them a compliance letter stating that their backfilling violated the CWA because the land contained protected wetlands.[6] The EPA warned there would be a $40,000 penalty if the Sacketts continued the project.[7]

At the time, the EPA interpreted the "waters of the United States" to include all waters that "could affect interstate or foreign commerce," as well as wetlands "adjacent to" those waters.[8] The agency instructed its officials "to assert jurisdiction over wetlands 'adjacent' to non-navigable tributaries when those wetlands had 'a significant nexus to traditional navigable waters.'"[9] "A 'significant nexus' existed when 'wetlands either alone or in combination with *similarly situated lands* in the region *significantly affected* the chemical, physical and biological integrity' of those waters."[10]

In this case, the EPA stated that the Sackett's lot was adjacent to an unnamed tributary on the other side of a 30-foot road because the wetlands and the tributary were in the same neighborhood.[11] The tributary feeds into a non-navigable creek that feeds into Priest Lake, an intrastate body of water designated by the EPA as traditionally navigable.[12] Therefore, the EPA concluded the Sacketts illegally dumped soil and gravel onto the "waters of the United States."[13]

The Sacketts brought a lawsuit under the Administrative Procedure Act, alleging that the EPA lacked jurisdiction because any wetlands on their property were not "waters of the United States."[14]

The Meaning of "Waters of the United States"

The Clean Water Act speaks of "navigable waters," which are defined in 33 U.S.C. § 1362(7) as "the waters of the United States." In *Rapanos v. United States*, a plurality concluded that the Clean Water Act applies to two categories of water: "certain relatively permanent bodies of water connected to traditional interstate navigable waters" and "wetlands with such a close physical connection to those waters that they were 'as practical matter indistinguishable from waters of the United States.'"[15]

The Court had previously held that the use of "navigable" implies that the definition refers mainly to bodies of water such as rivers, lakes, and oceans.[16] Justice Alito wrote that the Clean Water Act's "use of 'waters' encompasses only those relatively permanent, standing or continuously flowing bodies of water 'forming geographical features' that are described in ordinary parlance as 'streams, oceans, rivers, and lakes.'"[17]

The Court rejected the EPA's argument that "waters" is "naturally read to encompass wetlands" because the "presence of water is 'universally regarded as the most basic feature of wetlands.'"[18] Rejecting this argument, the Court pointed to "puddles," which are also defined by the "ordinary presence of water," even though few would describe puddles as "waters."[19] The Court held that for wetlands to qualify as "waters of the United States," they must be "indistinguishably part of a body of water that itself constitutes 'waters' under the CWA."[20] And the Court explained that "[w]etlands that are separate from traditional navigable waters cannot be considered part of those waters, even if they are located nearby."[21]

The Court stressed that if it accepted the EPA's definition, the EPA would have control over almost all land in the United States, infringing on state power.[22] The Court stated it requires "Congress to enact exceedingly clear language if it wishes to significantly alter the balance between federal and state power and the power of government over property."[23]

The Court also raised concerns over vagueness. The Clean Water Act includes criminal penalties. Due process requires Congress to define penal statutes with "sufficient definiteness that ordinary people can understand" and in a way that prevents "arbitrary and discriminatory enforcement."[24] The Court said that the EPA's proposed broad definition would be too vague and, therefore, potentially violate due process.[25]

The wetlands on the Sackett's property are distinguishable from "waters of the United States." The Court followed the plurality opinion in *Rapanos v. United States* and declared that the CWA "extends to only those wetlands with a continuous surface connection to bodies that are waters of the United States in their own right," so that they are "indistinguishable from those waters."[26] The Court thus concluded that the wetlands on the Sacketts' property are not within the scope of the Clean Water Act.[27]

There were several separate opinions. Justice Thomas, joined by Justice Gorsuch, wrote to discuss the meaning of "navigable waters" within the Clean Water Act. He said the Act was adopted under Congress's commerce power and is therefore limited to what can be regulated under that authority. He noted, "The history of federal regulation of navigable waters demonstrates that Congress' authority over navigation, as traditionally understood, was narrow but deep. It only applied to a discrete set of navigable waters and could only be used to keep those waters open for interstate commerce."[28]

Justice Thomas rejected the EPA's broad definition of navigable waters as giving it too much authority over matters traditionally regulated by the states. He wrote: "If this interpretation were correct, the only prudent move for any landowner in America would be to ask the Federal Government for permission before undertaking any kind of development. This regime turns Congress' traditionally limited navigation authority on its head. The baseline under the Constitution, the CWA, and the Court's precedents is state control of waters."[29]

Interestingly, Justice Thomas used his dissent to renew his objection to a broad view of Congress's commerce power. He said that the broad application of the Clean Water Act is "indicative of deeper problems with the Court's Commerce Clause jurisprudence."[30] He repeated his view that the commerce clause should be read narrowly as giving Congress power only to regulate "selling, buying, and bartering, as well as transporting for these purposes."[31] This is a rejection of the broad view of the commerce power that the Court has taken since 1937 and would make countless federal laws unconstitutional, including most federal environmental laws.

Justice Kagan wrote an opinion concurring in the judgment that took a very different approach. Joined by Justices Sotomayor and Jackson. She wrote: "The majority's 'continuous surface connection' test disregards the ordinary meaning of 'adjacent.' The majority thus alters—more precisely, narrows the scope of—the statute Congress drafted."[32] Justice Kagan stressed the broad scope intended by Congress for the Clean Water Act and said that the Court was abandoning this and not following the text of the statute. She said that the majority was "wrong" and declared: "'Adjacent' means neighboring, whether or not touching; so, for example, a wetland is adjacent to water on the other side of a sand dune. That congressional judgment is as clear as clear can be—which is to say, as clear as language gets."[33] She concluded by lamenting "the Court's appointment of itself as the national decision-maker on environmental policy."[34]

Justice Kavanaugh wrote an opinion concurring in the judgment, joined by Justices Sotomayor, Kagan, and Jackson. Although he agreed with the result, he disagreed with the Court's narrow interpretation of the Clean Water Act. He declared: "The Court's 'continuous surface connection' test departs from the statutory text, from 45 years of consistent agency practice, and from this Court's precedents. The Court's test narrows the Clean Water Act's coverage of 'adjacent' wetlands to mean only 'adjoining' wetlands. . . By narrowing the Act's coverage of wetlands to only adjoining wetlands, the Court's new test will leave some long-regulated adjacent wetlands no longer covered by the Clean Water Act, with significant repercussions for water quality and flood control throughout the United States."[35]

Implications

No doubt the Court's decision in *Sackett v. Environmental Protection Agency* narrows the application of the Clean Water Act. Congress could fix this by amending the statute, but until then, the Court's restrictive interpretation is controlling. The case also reflects underlying disagreements over the scope of federal power, the breadth of Congress's authority under the commerce clause, and how federal statutes should be interpreted. The unanimous result should not mask the serious disagreements among the justices on these issues and environmental law more generally.

Endnotes

1. 143 S. Ct. 1322 (2023).
2. *Id.* at 1329.
3. *Id.* at 1341.
4. *Id.*
5. *Id.* at 1331.
6. *Id.*
7. *Id.*

8. *Id.*
9. *Id.*
10. *Id.*
11. *Id.* at 1331–32.
12. *Id.* at 1332.
13. *Id.*
14. *Id.*
15. 547 U.S. 715, 742 (2006).
16. 143 S. Ct. 1322 at 1336–38.
17. *Id.* at 1336.
18. *Id.* at 1338.
19. *Id.*
20. *Id.* at 1339.
21. *Id.* at 1340.
22. *Id.* at 1341.
23. *Id.*
24. *Id.* at 1342.
25. *Id.*
26. *Id.* at 1344.
27. *Id.*
28. *Id.* at 1348 (Thomas, J., concurring).
29. *Id.* at 1357 (Thomas, J., concurring) (internal citation omitted).
30. *Id.* at 1358 (Thomas, J., concurring).
31. *See Gonzales v. Raich*, 545 U.S. 1, 58–59 (2005) (Thomas, J., dissenting).
32. 143 S. Ct. 1322 at 1359 (Kagan, J., concurring in the judgment).
33. *Id.* at 1361 (Kagan, J., concurring in the judgment).
34. *Id.* at 1361–62 (Kagan, J., concurring in the judgment).
35. *Id.* at 1362 (Kavanaugh, J., concurring in the judgment).

8

Executive Power and State Challenges to It

In recent years, as the country has become ever more politically polarized, there has been a proliferation of suits by states that disagree with presidential choices. Blue states, including California, brought suits during the Trump administration, and these suits have increased with conservative states taking the Biden administration to court.

Two important cases involving state challenges to Biden administration policies came to the Court in October Term 2022. In one, *United States v. Texas*, the Court dismissed a suit by state governments challenging the Biden administration's priorities with regard to arresting and deporting undocumented individuals for lack of standing.[1] In the other, *Biden v. Nebraska*, the Court found that states had standing to challenge the Biden administration's student loan forgiveness program and the Court invalidated the program.[2] In an opinion by Chief Justice Roberts, the Court said that whether to give such loan forgiveness is a "major question" of economic and political significance and that Congress had not been sufficiently specific in granting the President the authority to provide such relief.

These cases make clear that the Court will treat state governments as litigants under the same standing rules that it applies to all others suing in federal court. It is also apparent—as it was last term in *West Virginia v. EPA*[3]—that the major questions doctrine is a significant, though still relatively undefined, limit on executive power.

United States v. Texas

In 2021, the Biden administration's Department of Homeland Security announced its priorities in arresting and deporting those who are illegally in the United States. There are over 11 million undocumented individuals in the country, but at most only several hundred thousand are deported each year.[4] Therefore, the Biden administration said that it would prioritize arresting and deporting those unlawfully present who are suspected terrorists or dangerous criminals or who have unlawfully entered the country only recently.

Texas and Louisiana sued the Department of Homeland Security in federal court claiming that federal laws require the federal government to arrest more noncitizens pending their deportation. As Justice Brett Kavanaugh said, "The States essentially want the Federal Judiciary to order the Executive Branch to alter its arrest policy so as to make more arrests."[5]

The lawsuit reflects deep political disagreements over immigration policies. The federal district court and the United States Court of Appeals for the Fifth Circuit ruled that the states could sue in federal court because they incurred additional costs from the presence of undocumented individuals.

However, the Supreme Court in an 8–1 decision ruled that the states lacked standing to sue in federal court. Justice Kavanaugh wrote the opinion for the Court. Justice Alito was the sole dissenter.

Justice Kavanaugh said that there is not standing to challenge enforcement priorities of the executive branch of government. He wrote: "The States have not cited any precedent, history, or tradition of courts ordering the Executive Branch to change its arrest or prosecution policies so that the Executive Branch makes more arrests or initiates more prosecutions. On the contrary, this Court has previously ruled that a plaintiff lacks standing to bring such a suit."[6]

The Court focused on its precedent from 1973 in *Linda R.S. v. Richard D.*[7] A woman challenged the Texas policy of not prosecuting unmarried fathers for their failure to pay child support. The Supreme Court ruled that she lacked standing to sue. Justice Kavanaugh said that the "Court's Article III holding in *Linda R. S.* applies to challenges to the Executive Branch's exercise of enforcement discretion over whether to arrest or prosecute."[8] The Court stressed that this is particularly important in the context of immigration policy where there is great deference to the executive branch of government. Justice Kavanaugh declared: "That principle of enforcement discretion over arrests and prosecutions extends to the immigration context, where the Court has stressed that the Executive's enforcement discretion implicates not only 'normal domestic law enforcement priorities' but also 'foreign-policy objectives.'"[9] The Court explained that allowing standing would put the Court in the untenable position of overseeing the enforcement priorities of the executive branch of government.

Justice Kavanaugh concluded his majority opinion: "In sum, the States have brought an extraordinarily unusual lawsuit. They want a federal court to order the Executive Branch to alter its arrest policies so as to make more arrests. Federal courts have not traditionally entertained that kind of lawsuit; indeed, the States cite no precedent for a lawsuit like this. The States lack Article III standing because this Court's precedents and the 'historical experience' preclude the States' 'attempt to litigate this dispute at this time and in this form.'"[10]

Justice Gorsuch, joined by Justices Thomas and Barrett, concurred in the judgment. They also found a lack of standing but by focusing on "redressability."[11] It is well established that, in order for a plaintiff to have standing, he or she must have suffered an injury (or be imminently likely to suffer one) that was caused by the defendant and that is likely to be redressed by a favorable court decision. Justice Gorsuch stressed that even if the Court ruled in favor of Texas and Louisiana, it is quite uncertain that there would be more arrests and deportations or how anything would change for the states.

Justice Barrett also concurred in the judgment, joined by Justice Gorsuch, and she, too, emphasized redressability. She wrote: "The States failed to show that the District Court could order effective relief. And because redressability is an essential element of Article III standing, the District Court did not have jurisdiction."[12]

Only Justice Alito dissented. He argued that the states were economically injured by the failure of the federal government to enforce immigration laws. He said that the states alleged harms that were caused by the defendants and that there would likely be remedies provided by a favorable court decision. He expressed disagreement with the Court's refusal to hear the states' claim and saw it as undermining separation of powers. He wrote: "Congress enacted a law that requires the apprehension and detention of certain illegal aliens whose release, it thought, would endanger public safety. The Secretary of DHS does not agree with that categorical requirement. He prefers a more flexible policy. And the Court's answer today is that the Executive's policy choice prevails unless Congress, by withholding funds, refusing to confirm Presidential nominees, threatening impeachment and removal, etc., can win a test of strength." Justice Alito disagreed and said: "Relegating Congress to these disruptive measures radically alters the balance of power between Congress and the Executive, as well as the allocation of authority between the Congress that enacts a law and a later Congress that must go to war with the Executive if it wants that law to be enforced."[13]

The core of the Court's analysis is its recognition that inevitably the government must make choices in enforcing the law. Thankfully, not every law is enforced all of the time. Police do not arrest everyone going a mile over the speed limit. Possession of even a small amount of marijuana is a federal crime, but rarely does the federal government prosecute that. The Supreme Court recognized that the Department of Homeland Security must set priorities in arresting and deporting noncitizens and it is not for the federal courts to second guess those choices. As Justice Kavanaugh wrote, "If the Court green-lighted this suit, we could anticipate complaints in future years about alleged Executive Branch under-enforcement of any similarly worded laws—whether they be drug laws, gun laws, obstruction of justice laws, or the like. We decline to start the Federal Judiciary down that uncharted path."[14]

The greatest significance of the decision is in the Court restricting the ability of states to sue when they dislike federal policy. But the Court did not close the door to all suits by states. It simply said that for a state to sue it must meet the traditional requirements imposed on all civil litigation in federal court: the state must show that it was directly harmed, that the defendant caused the harm, and that a favorable federal court ruling can remedy the harm. This is the rule that has been followed for decades and the Court applied it to dismiss the suit by Texas and Louisiana against the Biden administration.

Biden v. Nebraska

A federal statute, the Higher Education Relief Opportunities for Students Act of 2003 (HEROES Act), explicitly authorizes the Secretary of Education to "waive or modify" student loan obligations in an emergency. President Biden invoked this authority to create a loan forgiveness program that benefits most with student loans. But the Supreme Court, in a 6–3 decision, ruled that he lacked authority under the law to take this step, a step that would help more than 43 million people.

In the early days of the COVID pandemic, then President Trump used the authority under this statute to suspend the need for most borrowers to repay student loan obligations. President Biden, on taking office, continued this relief. He then made it permanent, providing up to $20,000 of forgiveness of student loans for those who qualified.

Two lawsuits were filed challenging this action. One was brought by two individuals who did not qualify for relief under the Biden program. The Supreme Court, in *Department of Education v. Brown*,[15] unanimously found that the two individuals lacked standing to sue because striking down the Biden program would not benefit them. They still would not end up with loan forgiveness. Moreover, their claim that the Biden administration did not follow proper procedures was not linked to any injury they could demonstrate.

But in the other case—*Biden v. Nebraska*—the Supreme Court, in a 6–3 decision, invalidated Biden's loan forgiveness program. As in *United States v. Texas*, there was a question of whether state governments had standing to sue.

Chief Justice Roberts, writing for the Court, found that Missouri had standing to sue and that was sufficient for the justices to consider the merits of the case. He focused on an agency in Missouri, the Missouri Higher Education Loan Authority, that was created to help state residents obtain student loans for college. The Court noted that the Biden plan would provide debt relief to more than half of people with student loans and that the plan could cost the agency as much as $44 million a year. The Court stated: "The plan's harm to MOHELA is also a harm to Missouri. MOHELA is a 'public instrumentality' of the State."[16] He explained: "By law and function, MOHELA is an instrumentality of Missouri: It was created by the State to further a public purpose, is governed by state officials and state appointees, reports to the State, and may be dissolved by the State. The Secretary's plan will cut MOHELA's revenues, impairing its efforts to aid Missouri college students. This acknowledged harm to MOHELA in the performance of its public function is necessarily a direct injury to Missouri itself."[17]

Justice Kagan, in a dissent joined by Justices Sotomayor and Jackson, strongly disagreed that Missouri had standing. She said that the injury was to MOHELA, which is an independent entity that was not a party to the lawsuit. She wrote: "The plaintiffs in this case are six States that have no personal stake in the Secretary's loan forgiveness plan. They are classic ideological plaintiffs: They think the plan a very bad idea, but they are no worse off because the Secretary differs. In giving those States a forum—in adjudicating their complaint—the Court forgets its proper role. The Court acts as though it is an arbiter of political and policy disputes, rather than of cases and controversies."[18]

Having found standing, the Court reached the merits and struck down the Biden debt relief program. The central question was whether the HEROES Act, which permits the Secretary of Education to "waive or modify" student loan obligations in an emergency, provided authority for the Biden action. Chief Justice Roberts said that this extensive debt relief is much more than a "modification." As to "waiver," he said that this is much more than has ever been done before.

The Court then invoked the "major questions doctrine," the principle that a federal agency cannot act on a major question of economic or political significance unless it has clear direction from Congress. Chief Justice Roberts said whether the Secretary of Education can give this loan relief is a major question and that Congress was not sufficiently specific in authorizing such relief. He noted: "The 'economic and political significance' of the Secretary's action is staggering by any measure. Practically every student borrower benefits, regardless of circumstances. A budget model issued by the Wharton School of the University of Pennsylvania estimates that the program will cost taxpayers 'between $469 billion and $519 billion,' depending on the total number of borrowers ultimately covered."[19]

The Court said that when there is such a major question, the President must "point to 'clear congressional authorization' to justify the challenged program."[20] The Court said that none existed here.

Justice Barrett wrote a concurring opinion to clarify her understanding of the major questions doctrine. She said that "the doctrine serves as an interpretive tool reflecting common sense as to the manner in which Congress is likely to delegate a policy decision of such economic and political magnitude to an administrative agency."[21] For her, the major questions doctrine focuses on whether the agency has gone beyond the bounds of the authority delegated by Congress.

Justice Kagan wrote a scathing dissent. In addition to disputing whether there was standing, she said that the statutory language is clear: the Secretary of Education can "waive" student loan obligations. One of the most basic principles of interpretation is that the text of a law should be followed unless it is unconstitutional.

The dissent also objected to the major questions doctrine. As she did in a dissent a year ago in *West Virginia v. EPA*, Justice Kagan sharply criticized the major questions doctrine as lacking foundation in the law and being inappropriately used to challenge congressional delegation of power. Justice Kagan wrote: "The opinion ends by applying the Court's made-up major-questions doctrine to jettison the Secretary's loan forgiveness plan. Small wonder the majority invokes the doctrine. The majority's "normal" statutory interpretation cannot sustain its decision. The statute, read as written, gives the Secretary broad authority to relieve a national emergency's effect on borrowers' ability to repay their student loans. The Secretary did no more than use that lawfully delegated authority. So the majority applies a rule specially crafted to kill significant regulatory action, by requiring Congress to delegate not just clearly but also micro-specifically."[22]

This case is important on many levels. As for standing, it indicates that state governments can sue whenever there is an injury to a state agency, however independent. As for challenges to federal agency actions, the

Court invokes the relatively newly minted "major questions doctrine." It remains unclear what is a major question of economic or political significance, or what is sufficient congressional specificity to satisfy the Court. It thus has opened the door to challenges to a plethora of agency actions on the grounds that they involve major questions and Congress was not sufficiently specific in its statutory authorization. And as for practical consequences, 43 million people who would have received debt relief will no longer get it.

Endnotes

1. 143 S. Ct. 1964 (2023).
2. 143 S. Ct. 2355 (2023).
3. 142 S. Ct. 2587 (2022).
4. Elma Mrkonji, *37+ Remarkable Deportation Statistics [The View from 2021]* (Jun. 30, 2021), https://thehighcourt.co/deportation-statistics/
5. 143 S. Ct. 1964 at 1968.
6. *Id.* at 1970.
7. *Linda R. S. v. Richard D.*, 410 U.S. 614 (1973)
8. 143 S. Ct. 1964 at 1970.
9. *Id.* at 1971.
10. *Id.* at 1976.
11. *Id.* at 1976 (Gorsuch, J., concurring in the judgment).
12. *Id.* at 1986 (Barrett, J., concurring in the judgment).
13. *Id.* at 2002 (Alito, J., dissenting).
14. *Id.* at 1973.
15. 143 S. Ct. 2342 (2003).
16. 143 S. Ct. 2355 (2023).
17. *Id.* at 2366.
18. *Id.* at 2381 (Kagan, J., dissenting).
19. *Id.* at 2373.
20. *Id.* at 2375.
21. *Id.* at 2378 (Barrett, J., concurring).
22. *Id.* at 2400 (Kagan, J., dissenting).

9

Freedom of Speech

October Term 2022 was an important one for freedom of speech. In *303 Creative LLC v. Elenis*, the Supreme Court held that freedom of expression provides a basis for an exemption from a state antidiscrimination law.[1] In *Counterman v. Colorado*, the Court clarified the definition of a "true threat," which is unprotected by the First Amendment.[2] And in *Twitter v. Taamneh*,[3] the Supreme Court rejected claims against social media companies for supporting terrorist activity.[4]

303 Creative LLC v. Elenis

When does the First Amendment provide a constitutional basis for violation of state (or even federal) antidiscrimination laws? That was the issue in *303 Creative LLC v. Elenis*, and the Supreme Court held that when an individual is engaged in expressive activity, he or she has the right to refuse to provide services even when it otherwise would violate antidiscrimination laws.[5] This is an important ruling that is likely to spawn a great deal of litigation over when someone is engaged in expressive activity and therefore has a First Amendment right to discriminate.

Lorie Smith, a graphic artist and web designer, wanted to design websites for weddings but refused to do so for same-sex weddings because of her religious beliefs. She particularly objected to the idea of providing same-sex couples with the original content that she planned for her wedding websites to feature. Colorado law prohibits businesses that sell or offer services "to the public" from discriminating based on "disability, race, creed, color, sex, sexual orientation, marital status, national origin, or ancestry."

Smith filed a lawsuit in federal district court to have the law declared unconstitutional as applied to her and for an injunction to keep it from being enforced against her. She has not yet begun designing websites for weddings but wanted the law clarified before she took the risk of violating the law. Interestingly, after the Supreme Court decided the case, there were stories in the media that the affidavits that she relied on of same-sex couples that requested her services were false.[6] This, however, does not undermine the precedential value of the decision; a final judgment cannot later be attacked for lack of jurisdiction.

The federal district court and the United States Court of Appeals for the Tenth Circuit rejected these claims and stressed that the government has a compelling interest in preventing discrimination based on sexual orientation. The Supreme Court granted review on the free speech issue but not on the question concerning free exercise of religion. This is important because the decision will apply to anyone who is engaged in expressive activity and has a conscientious objection to providing service; it is not limited to those whose religious beliefs are the basis for their discrimination.

Smith argued that the Colorado law impermissibly compels her speech by requiring that she design websites for same-sex couples. But the State of Colorado argued that the state is regulating conduct—prohibiting discriminatory conduct—and only incidentally controlling Smith's speech. The underlying issue is of enormous importance: does the First Amendment provide a basis for exemptions from antidiscrimination laws?

The Supreme Court, in a 6–3 decision written by Justice Gorsuch, ruled in favor of Smith. He reviewed the Supreme Court's precedents concerning compelled speech and declared: "the First Amendment protects an individual's right to speak his mind regardless of whether the government considers his speech sensible and well intentioned or deeply 'misguided,' and likely to cause 'anguish' or 'incalculable grief.' Equally, the First Amendment protects acts of expressive association. Generally, too, the government may not compel a person to speak its own preferred messages."[7]

The Court adopted Smith's argument that applying the Colorado law to her would be impermissible compelled speech. She would be forced by the Colorado law to design websites, and all the speech that entailed, against her wishes and her beliefs. Justice Gorsuch stated: "Taken seriously, that principle would allow the government to force all manner of artists, speechwriters, and others whose services involve speech to speak what they do not believe on pain of penalty. The government could require 'an unwilling Muslim movie director to make a film with a Zionist message,' or 'an atheist muralist to accept a commission celebrating Evangelical zeal,' so long as they would make films or murals for other members of the public with different messages. Equally, the government could force a male website designer married to another man to design websites for an organization that advocates against same-sex marriage."[8]

The case thus means that a person can refuse to provide services even though it violates antidiscrimination laws if the individual is engaged in expressive activity. A crucial question in future litigation will be what constitutes expressive activity. As to this, Justice Gorsuch wrote simply: "Doubtless, determining what qualifies as expressive activity protected by the First Amendment can sometimes raise difficult questions. But this case presents no complication of that kind."[9]

Justice Sotomayor wrote a vehement dissent, joined by Justices Kagan and Jackson. She stressed the importance of public accommodations laws that prohibit discrimination on the basis of race, sex, religion, and sexual orientation. She rejected the argument that the law compelled Smith to provide service to anyone. Smith did not have to design websites for weddings, but if she did offer her services to the public then she should not be able to discriminate based on sexual orientation. Justice Sotomayor wrote: "the law in question targets conduct, not speech, for regulation, and the *act* of discrimination has never constituted protected expression under the First Amendment. Our Constitution contains no right to refuse service to a disfavored group."[10]

The dissent stressed the compelling government interest served by public accommodations laws that prohibit discrimination. Justice Sotomayor powerfully declared: "Today is a sad day in American constitutional law and in the lives of LGBT people. The Supreme Court of the United States declares that a particular kind of business, though open to the public, has a constitutional right to refuse to serve members of a protected class. The Court does so for the first time in its history."[11]

There always is a tension between liberty and equality. Any law that prohibits discrimination limits the freedom to discriminate. For decades, the Supreme Court held that stopping discrimination is more important than the freedom to discriminate. Now, though, the Court has found a First Amendment right to discriminate.

It is crucial to keep in mind that this case is not focused on religious beliefs; anyone who has a conscientious objection to providing services may refuse to do so if it involves expressive activity. Simply put, this means that anyone can violate state antidiscrimination laws if they claim that they are engaged in expressive activity. In the wedding context, it likely means that bakers who design cakes, florists who make floral arrangements, engravers who prepare invitations, and videographers and photographers all can refuse to serve customers notwithstanding laws prohibiting discrimination.

But this extends beyond the wedding context to all work. Anyone engaged in expressive activity now has a First Amendment right to refuse to provide service. Most work can be said to involve expressive activity. Those who cook food, sew clothes, design cabinets, to mention a few examples, would claim that they are engaged in expressive activity.

Moreover, all laws that prohibit discrimination compel association. That was long the basis for opposition to antidiscrimination laws: that people have the right to choose who to serve and who to associate with. Prior to *303 Creative LLC v. Elenis*, the Court had rejected that argument. Its significance is in its finding a First Amendment right to discrimination, in violation of antidiscrimination laws, when there is expressive activity.

Counterman v. Colorado

Over a half century ago, in *United States v. Watts* (1969), the Supreme Court held that true threats are speech unprotected by the First Amendment.[12] Robert Watts, then 18, declared at a public rally that, "I have already received my draft classification as 1-A and I have got to report for my physical this Monday coming. I am not going. If they ever make me carry a rifle the first man I want to get in my sights is L.B.J." Watts was arrested and convicted for violating a federal law that makes it a crime to "knowingly and willfully" threaten the life of the President.[13]

The Supreme Court upheld the federal statute, but reversed Watts' conviction. The Court reasoned that although true threats are unprotected by the First Amendment, they must be distinguished from speech that is merely hyperbole. The Court concluded that Watts' statement was "political hyperbole."[14]

In subsequent cases, the Court reaffirmed that true threats are not protected by the First Amendment, but it never articulated the standard for determining what constitutes a true threat under the First Amendment.[15] As the Court noted there are "high First Amendment stakes" because the standard for determining true threats determines when people can be punished or held liable for their speech.[16]

The lower courts across the country divided between two major approaches to defining what is a true threat. Some state and federal courts, including the Colorado Supreme Court, employed an objective test: speech is unprotected if it would cause a reasonable person to feel threatened.[17] Their view is that there is no constitutional right to make another person fear for his or her physical safety.

But other courts adopted a subjective approach, holding that the First Amendment requires that there be a subjective intent to threaten in order to punish a person for speech.[18] This is a much harder standard to meet—and thus more protective of speech—because of the difficulty of proving a person's intentions.

In *Counterman v. Colorado*, the Court clarified the definition of a true threat and adopted neither the objective nor the subjective approach, instead focusing on "recklessness" as the appropriate legal standard.[19] The case involved Billy Raymond Counterman, who for over two years sent hundreds of messages over Facebook to a singer, identified as "C.W." Sometimes the messages were conversational about his life; sometimes they expressed anger towards C.W. She felt in danger and canceled concerts and took safety precautions. She never responded to Counterman's messages and, when she came to feel threatened and feared for her safety, she filed a report with the police.

Counterman was prosecuted under a Colorado law that provides for criminal liability if speech "would cause a reasonable person to suffer serious emotional distress."[20] The Colorado Supreme Court previously had held that conviction requires proof only that the speaker "knowingly" make repeated communications and does not "require that a perpetrator be aware that his or her acts would cause a reasonable person to suffer serious emotional distress."[21] Counterman was convicted and sentenced to four and a half years in prison.

The Supreme Court, in an opinion by Justice Kagan, reversed the Colorado courts and sent the case back to apply the new legal standard: a speaker can be punished if he "consciously disregarded a substantial risk that his communication would be viewed a threat of violence."[22] The Court rejected the subjective standard as not providing enough protection of safety and the objective standard as not doing enough to safeguard speech. Thus, the issue on remand is whether Counterman consciously disregarded a substantial risk that his communication would be perceived as a threat.

Justice Kagan's opinion reviewed other areas of law where a recklessness standard is used, particularly defamation law. Under *New York Times Co. v. Sullivan*, a public official can recover for defamation by proving both that the statement is false and that the speaker acted with reckless disregard of the truth.[23]

Justice Kagan expressly recognized that her approach is a compromise between a subjective approach more protective of speech and an objective approach more protective of safety. As she explained: "That standard, again, is recklessness. It offers 'enough "breathing space" for protected speech,' without sacrificing too many of the benefits of enforcing laws against true threats. As with any balance, something is lost on both sides: The rule we adopt today is neither the most speech-protective nor the most sensitive to the dangers of true threats."[24]

Justice Sotomayor concurred in the judgment, joined by Justice Gorsuch.[25] Although they agreed with the outcome in this case, they disagreed that recklessness generally should be the standard in true threats cases. They expressed concern that this approach is not sufficiently speech protective. Justice Sotomayor wrote: "Where I part ways with the Court is that I would not reach the distinct and more complex question whether a *mens rea* of recklessness is sufficient for true-threats prosecutions generally. Further, requiring nothing more than a *mens rea* of recklessness is inconsistent with precedent, history, and the commitment to even harmful speech that the First Amendment enshrines."[26]

Justice Barrett, joined by Justice Thomas, dissented. The dissenters would have affirmed the lower courts, used their objective test for determining what is a true threat, and upheld Counterman's conviction. Justice Barrett explained: "True threats carry little value and impose great cost. '[B]y their very utterance,' true threats 'inflict injury.' They provoke 'the fear of violence,' create 'disruption,' give rise to 'the possibility that the threatened violence will occur'—and the list goes on. The nature of a true threat points to an objective test for determining the scope of First Amendment protection: Neither its 'social value' nor its potential for 'injury' depends on the speaker's subjective intent."[27]

Justice Thomas wrote separately to reiterate his view that *New York Times v. Sullivan*—the landmark case concerning First Amendment limits on defamation liability—was wrongly decided and should be overruled.[28] Justice Thomas raised this because the majority opinion had approvingly cited that precedent in justifying a recklessness standard for determining what is a true threat.

Because of the internet and social media, there are far more instances of speech that can be regarded as true threats and, therefore, many more criminal prosecutions and civil suits based on such speech. *Counterman v. Colorado* offers much needed clarification for when speech can be regarded as a true threat unprotected by the First Amendment.

Twitter v. Tamneh and *Gonzalez v. Google*

Sometimes there is great significance in what the Court *doesn't* do, as exemplified by two cases the Court handed down about the internet and social media. In *Twitter v. Tamneh* and *Gonzalez v. Google*, the Court unanimously rejected holding internet and social media companies liable for aiding and abetting terrorist activities for what was posted on their platforms. A contrary ruling would have engendered a huge amount of litigation and changed how the internet functions. Although many questions remain open, these rulings reflect justices who understandably want to be cautious as to the judicial role in setting policy for the internet and social media.

The issue in *Twitter v. Tamneh* is whether social media platforms can be held liable for aiding and abetting terrorist activity for content posted on their websites.[29] In an opinion by Justice Clarence Thomas, the Court emphatically rejected such liability.

The case arose from a terrorist attack on the Reina nightclub in Istanbul, Turkey, in the early hours of January 1, 2017. The attack was carried out by Abdulkadir Masharipov on behalf of the Islamic State of Iraq and Syria (ISIS). Masharipov entered the nightclub and fired more than 120 rounds into a crowd of more than 700 people, killing 39 people and injuring 60 others.

The family of someone killed in the attack, Nawras Alassaf, sued Facebook, Inc., Google, Inc., and Twitter, Inc., claiming that they aided and abetted ISIS and thus were liable for the Reina nightclub attack. The plaintiffs claimed that ISIS and its adherents use these platforms as tools for recruiting, fundraising, and spreading their propaganda. The plaintiffs alleged that these platforms have been crucial to ISIS spreading its message of terror and gaining new members. Further, the plaintiffs claimed that these social media companies knew that ISIS used their platforms and therefore aided and abetted terrorist activity.

Federal law 18 U. S. C. § 2333 allows United States nationals who have been "injured . . . by reason of an act of international terrorism" to sue for damages. The law imposes civil liability on "any person who aids and abets, by knowingly providing substantial assistance, or who conspires with the person who committed such an act of international terrorism."[30] Under this provision, victims of terrorist acts therefore may seek to recover from those who aided and abetted the terrorist act that injured them.

The Supreme Court said that the concept of "aiding and abetting" long has existed in the law and must be confined to limit who can be held liable. Justice Thomas explained, "To keep aiding-and-abetting liability grounded in culpable misconduct, criminal law thus requires 'that a defendant in some sort associate himself with the venture, that he participate in it as in something that he wishes to bring about, that he seek by his action to make it succeed' before he could be held liable."[31] There must be some "culpable conduct" by the defendant, an "affirmative act with the intent of facilitating the offense's commission."

The Court applied this standard to conclude that the social media platforms could not be held liable for the terrorist attack that occurred in Turkey. The Court explained that in no way did these platforms "associate" themselves with the shooting. The Court observed, "Notably, plaintiffs never allege that ISIS used defendants' platforms to plan or coordinate the Reina attack; in fact, they do not allege that Masharipov himself ever used Facebook, YouTube, or Twitter."[32] The relationship between the social media platforms and the terrorist attack was "too attenuated." In the Court's eyes, allowing liability would be no different from holding cellphone companies liable because of crimes plotted over cellphones.

The Court left open the possibility that there might be situations were social media platforms were more involved in criminal activity and could be held liable: "There may be, for example, situations where the provider of routine services does so in an unusual way or provides such dangerous wares that selling those goods to a terrorist group could constitute aiding and abetting a foreseeable terror attack." This would require "aid that is more direct, active, and substantial."[33] Put another way, merely being the place where material is posted is not enough to be a basis for aiding and abetting liability.

The factual context of *Gonzalez v. Google* was similar to that in *Twitter v. Tamneh*, but the legal issue was different.[34] An ISIS attack in Paris in 2015 killed 130 people, including Nohemi Gonzalez. Her parents sued Google under the federal statute creating liability for aiding and abetting terrorist activity. Google raised a defense under 47 U.S.C. § 230, which protects internet and social media companies from liability for content posted to their platforms by users and the platforms' decisions to remove (or not remove) that content.

Section 230 has been widely regarded as crucial for the development of the internet and social media. Jeff Kosseff, in the title of his book, described these as "the twenty-six words that created the internet."[35] It is hard to see how the internet and social media could function if platforms were held liable for what was posted or what was taken down.

The issue in *Gonzalez v. Google* is whether a social media platform loses its Section 230 protection because it uses algorithms to direct users' attention to particular content. As some of the justices expressed at oral argument, allowing such liability would open the door to a tremendous amount of litigation. The implications for the functioning of the internet and social media would be enormous because inevitably algorithms are used by social media companies in ordering and directing material.

The Court, in a per curiam opinion, ruled in favor of Google but without addressing the meaning of Section 230. The Court explained that under its holding in *Twitter v. Tamneh*, the allegations in the complaint were not sufficient to create a plausible claim for aiding and abetting liability. Therefore, there was no need to decide whether a defense was available under Section 230. The Court concluded, "We therefore decline to address the application of § 230 to a complaint that appears to state little, if any, plausible claim for relief."

The Court's decisions in these cases are significant because of what the Court did not do. It did not create liability for social media companies for what is posted on their platforms. Billions of things are posted on social media platforms every day. Allowing liability based on aiding and abetting liability would have engendered a huge change in how the internet and social media operate. The Supreme Court was not willing to open that door, at least based on the facts of these cases.

But these decisions are just the beginning of the Court having to consider how social media companies can be held accountable, whether via suits for money damages or by government regulation. There are petitions for certiorari pending in two cases likely to be heard next year—*Attorney General, Florida v. Netchoice, LLC* and *NetChoice, LLC v. Paxton*—that involve the constitutionality of state laws that prevent social media companies from engaging in content moderation.[36] And down the road are cases now pending in the lower court that involve challenges to state laws requiring more content moderation by social media platforms and that restrict access to them by minors. These cases, unlike *Twitter v. Tamneh* and *Gonzalez v. Google*, are likely to shape speech on the internet and social media for years to come.

Endnotes

1. 143 S. Ct. 2298 (2023).
2. 143 S. Ct. 2106 (2023).
3. 143 S. Ct. 1206 (2023).
4. 143 S. Ct. 1191 (2023).
5. 143 S. Ct. 2298 (2023).
6. *See* Colleen Slevin, et al. *The man named in the Supreme Court's gay rights ruling says he didn't request a wedding* website, AP News (June 30, 2023, 4:18 PM) https://apnews.com/article/supreme-court-gay-rights-lgbtq-website-385ec911ce0ca2f415966078eddb66da; *see also* Adam Liptak, *What to Know About the Seemingly Fake Document in a Gay Rights Case*, NY Times (July 3, 2023) https://www.nytimes.com/2023/07/03/us/politics/same-sex-marriage-document-supreme-court.html.
7. 143 S. Ct. 2298 at 2312.
8. *Id.* at 2314.
9. *Id.* at 2319.
10. *Id.* at 2322.
11. *Id.* at 2341.
12. 394 U.S. 705, 707 (1969).
13. *Id.* at 705.
14. *Id.* at 707.
15. Virginia v. Black, 538 U.S. 343, 347 (2003).
16. 143 S. Ct. 2106, 2114–15 (2023).
17. *See, e.g.*, People v. Baer, 973 P.2d 1225, 1233 (Colo. 1999); *see also, e.g.*, People v. Stanley, 170 P.3d 782, 787 (Colo. Ct. App. 2007).
18. *See, e.g.*, Rogers v. United States, 422 U.S. 35, 44 (1975); *see also, e.g.*, People ex. rel. R.D., 464 P.3d 717, 731 (2020).
19. 143 S. Ct. 2106 (2023).
20. *Id.* at 2112.
21. People v. Cross, 127 P.3d 71, 77 (Colo. 2006).
22. 143 S. Ct. 2106 at 2112.
23. 376 U.S. 254, 280 (1964).
24. 143 S. Ct. 2106 at 2119.
25. *Id.* at 2119 (Sotomayor, concurring in the judgment).
26. *Id.* at 2120.
27. *Id.* at 2134 (Barrett, J., dissenting).
28. *Id.* at 2132 (Thomas, J., dissenting); *see also, McKee v. Crosby*, 139 S. Ct. 675, 203 (opinion of Thomas, J.).
29. 143 S. Ct. 1206 (2023).
30. *Id.* at 1214.

31. *Id.* at 1221.
32. *Id.* at 1228.
33. *Id.*
34. 143 S. Ct. 1191 (2023).
35. *See generally*, JEFF KOSSEFF, THE TWENTY-SIX WORDS THAT CREATED THE INTERNET (2019).
36. 34 F.4th 1196, 1203 (11th Cir. 2022); 49 F.45th 439, 445 (5th Cir. 2022).

10

Immigration Law

Once more, this term, the Supreme Court sided with the United States in most of the cases concerning immigration law. As in past years, the Court gave great deference to the federal government.

In addition to the cases discussed below, in *United States v. Texas*—discussed in Chapter 7 on executive power—the Court dismissed a challenge by state governments to the Biden administration's priorities in arresting and deporting undocumented individuals.[1] The Court held that the states lacked standing to sue and thus did not reach the case's merits.

United States v. Hansen[2]

Federal law prohibits "encourage[ing] or induc[ing] a[] [non-citizen] to come to, enter, or reside in the United States, knowing or in reckless disregard of the fact that such coming to, entry, or residence is or will be in violation of the law."[3] The statute, by its very terms, is directed at speech. Does it violate the First Amendment?

In 2014, Helman Hansen ran a fraudulent "adult adoption" program that lured Mana Nailati, a Fijian, with the promise of United States citizenship.[4] Nailati and many others fell victim to Hansen's scam resulting in financial losses. In total, Hansen cheated his victims of nearly

$2 million.[5] The United States charged Hansen with several crimes, including violations of § 1324(a)(1)(A)(iv). Hansen attempted to have the charges dismissed as violating the First Amendment, arguing that the law is unconstitutionally overbroad.[6]

In a 7–2 decision, the Court rejected the challenge and upheld the law. Justice Barrett wrote the opinion for the Court, joined by Chief Justice Roberts and Justices Thomas, Alito, Kagan, Gorsuch, and Kavanaugh. The Court ruled that this provision of federal law "forbids only the intentional solicitation or facilitation of certain unlawful acts. It does not 'prohibi[t] a substantial amount of protected speech'—let alone enough to justify throwing out the law's 'plainly legitimate sweep.'"[7] Simply stated, the clause is not unconstitutionally overbroad.

Justice Barrett's opinion focused on the definitions of key words of the statute: "solicitation," "facilitation," "encourage," and "induce." She provides background on "solicitation" and "facilitation," defining each term through the Model Penal Code, a textbook, and various cases.[8] Justice Barrett then looks to the terms "encourage" and "induce," looking to several dictionaries, the federal criminal code, the Model Penal Code, and various state laws.[9] She finds that the "use of 'encourage' and 'induce' to describe solicitation and facilitation is both longstanding and pervasive."[10] The Court rejects Hansen's view that the 1952 and 1986 revisions demonstrate that Congress "opted to make 'protected speech, not conduct, a crime.'"[11] She says Congress simply "streamlined" the statutory language.[12]

The Court expressly rejected Hansen's claim that the statute "'prohibit[s] a substantial amount of speech' relative to its 'plainly legitimate sweep.'"[13] She argues that the clause's reach only extends to speech "integral to unlawful conduct."[14] Thus, the law is not unconstitutionally overbroad.

Justice Jackson wrote a dissent and focused on two points: (1) "the majority's interpretation of 8 U.S.C. § 1324(a)(1)(A) diverges from the text and history of the provision" and (2) the majority's interpretation "subverts the speech-protective goals of the constitutional doctrine."[15]

As to Justice Jackson's first point, she cites *United States v. Stevens* as to the standard for overbreadth: "A statute is overbroad—and thus facially invalid—if 'a substantial number of its applications are unconstitutional, judged in relation to the statute's plainly legitimate sweep.'"[16] Justice Jackson then applies the *Stevens* test to this case, finding § 1324(a)(1)(A) "unconstitutional as overbroad if it is read according to its plain text."[17] She underscores that the government does not challenge this claim.[18]

Justice Jackson then moves to dispute the majority's contention that § 1324(a)(1)(A) uses "encourage" and "induce" in a "specialized, criminal-law sense."[19] She argues that § 1324(a)(1)(A)'s use of "encourage or induce" is not synonymous with "solicits" or "facilitates" and does not incorporate the same features.[20] Justice Jackson then rejects the majority's statutory history argument, arguing that "Congress has sought to expand the reach of this criminal law."[21] She supports this claim by reviewing the same evidence as the majority and then looking at other features of § 1324(a)(1)(A).[22] In Justice Jackson's final section, she slams the majority for infringing the legislative domain and notes how this is especially worrisome in the context of a First Amendment challenge.[23]

Pugin v. Garland

Pugin v. Garland, which involves narrow questions of immigration law, produced a heated dissent and an unusual split among the justices.[24] Two cases that came to opposite conclusions—one from the Fourth Circuit and one from the Ninth Circuit—were consolidated before the Supreme Court.

Fernando Cordero-Garcia is a Mexican citizen convicted in 2009 of various California offenses, including dissuading a witness from reporting a crime.[25] Jean Francois Pugin is a Mauritian citizen who was convicted in 2014 of the Virginia offense of being an accessory after the fact to a felony.[26] The Department of Homeland Security found both noncitizens removable from the United States based on their convictions for aggravated felonies or offenses "relating to the obstruction of justice."[27] The Board of Immigration Appeals and an Immigration Judge ruled for the Department of Homeland Security in both cases.[28] Cordero-Garcia and Pugin appealed in their respective Court of Appeals. The Ninth Circuit concluded that Cordero-Garcia's conviction for dissuading a witness from reporting a crime did not qualify as an offense "relating to obstruction of justice" because California law did not require an ongoing investigation or proceeding.[29] But the Fourth Circuit held that Pugin's conviction for accessory after the fact qualified as an offense "relating to the obstruction of justice" regardless of a requirement for an ongoing investigation or proceeding.[30] The Court granted certiorari and consolidated the cases to resolve the circuit split.[31]

The issue before the Court was "whether an offense 'relat[es] to obstruction of justice' under § 1101(a)(43)(S) even if the offense does not require that an investigation or proceeding be *pending*."[32] This issue results because some obstruction offenses—like threatening a witness to prevent them from reporting a crime—occur regardless of an ongoing investigation or legal proceeding.[33]

Justice Kavanaugh wrote the opinion for the Court, joined by Chief Justice Roberts and Justices Thomas, Alito, Barrett, and Jackson. Justice Sotomayor wrote a vehement dissent, joined by Justices Kagan and Gorsuch. The Court held that an offense can "'relat[e] to the obstruction of justice' under § 1101(a)(43)(S) even if the offense does not require that investigation or proceeding be pending."[34] Additionally, under § 1227(a)(2)(A)(iii), noncitizens convicted of a federal or state crime classified as an "aggravated felony" can be removed from the United States.[35]

Under the Immigration and Nationality Act, noncitizens convicted of an "aggravated felony" can be removed from the United States.[36] The Act establishes that "aggravated felonies" encompass an array of federal and state crimes.[37] And, in 1996, Congress expanded "aggravated felony" to cover offenses "relating to the obstruction of justice, perjury or subornation of perjury, or bribery of a witness, for which the term of imprisonment is at least one year."[38] Justice Kavanaugh explains that the Supreme Court "has generally used the 'categorical approach' to determine whether a prior conviction qualifies as an 'aggravated felony' under § 1101(a)(43)."[39] Heeding this approach, courts turn to "the elements of the statute of conviction, not to the facts of each defendant's conduct," as the court's role is to establish which federal or state offenses "relat[e] to the obstruction of justice."[40] Justice Kavanaugh states that an offense "'relat[es] to the obstruction of justice' under § 1101(a)(43)(S) even if the offense does not require that an investigation or proceeding be *pending*" on three grounds.[41]

First, Justice Kavanaugh cites various sources such as dictionary definitions, federal laws, state laws, and the Model Penal Code to establish that obstruction offenses at either the federal or state level can be considered as "relating to obstruction of justice" under § 1101(a)(43)(S) whether or not the offense requires an ongoing investigation or legal proceeding.[42] Justice Kavanaugh cites dictionaries from the time when § 1101(a)(43)(S) was enacted in 1996 to provide evidence that obstruction of justice rarely demands the existence of a pending investigation or proceeding.[43] Justice Kavanaugh observes that these dictionary definitions lack the requirement of an ongoing investigation or proceeding. But he counters this by stating that these dictionaries show that obstruction of justice "*includes* offenses where an investigation or proceeding is pending, but is not *limited to* offenses where an investigation or proceeding is pending."[44] Lastly, Justice Kavanaugh cites the Model Penal Code, noting that it "generally does not require that an investigation or proceeding be pending."[45]

Second, Justice Kavanaugh states that this "extensive body of authority . . . reflects common sense. Individuals can obstruct the process of justice even when an investigation or proceeding is not pending."[46] In fact, obstructing justice is often "most effective" when it stops the investigations from starting.[47]

Third, Justice Kavanaugh holds that the use of the phrase "relating to" in the statute settles any ambiguity regarding § 1101(a)(43)(S)'s scope.[48] The phrase ensures that the statute covers offenses that have a connection with the obstruction of justice, including common obstruction offenses where there is no ongoing investigation or proceeding.[49] Justice Kavanaugh asserts that Congress did not use such broad language to define other aggravated felonies in this statute, and he juxtaposes this statute with 8 U.S.C. 1101(a)(43)(A), which just states "murder, rape, or sexual abuse of a minor."[50] He rejected invoking the rule of lenity, saying it does not apply here because the traditional methods of statutory interpretation establish that an offense "relating to obstruction of justice" does not require the existence of an ongoing investigation or proceeding.[51]

Justice Sotomayor wrote a heated dissent in which she proposed the opposite conclusion: "A reexamination of the sources relied upon by the majority, with the appropriate focus on discerning the trunk of obstruction of justice, rather than its various branches or offshoots, leads to the opposite result: To qualify as 'an offense relating to obstruction of justice' under § 1101(a)(43)(S), a predicate offense must require a pending investigation or proceeding."[52] She provides five grounds to support her argument.

First, Justice Sotomayor argues that the majority overlooks the fact that "obstruction of justice" was a well-established term of art when the statute was enacted in 1996.[53] Justice Sotomayor emphasizes that, historically, obstruction of justice has always required a pending investigation or proceeding.[54] Her dissent refers to early American laws and cases such as *Pettibone v. United States* to demonstrate that obstruction of justice is tied to the pendency of proceedings and the administration of justice.[55] She also points out that the modern obstruction of justice clause, which prohibits endeavors to obstruct the due administration of justice, reinforces this requirement.[56] She argues that Congress was aware of this settled interpretation when it added "obstruction of justice" to the list of aggravated felonies in the Immigration and Nationality Act (INA).[57]

Second, Justice Sotomayor cites the same authority as the majority (dictionary definitions, chapter 73 of the Federal Criminal Code, state statutes, and the Model Penal Code) to argue that "core obstruction of justice requires a pending investigation."[58] She examines these sources and comes to opposite conclusions from the majority.[59]

Third, Justice Sotomayor argues against the expansive interpretation of the phrase "relating to" in the statute.[60] She criticizes the majority's reading, stating that it disregards the statutory text and context of the phrase.[61] She suggests that a narrower interpretation should be adopted.[62] Justice Sotomayor points out that throughout the Immigration and Nationality Act, the phrase "relating to" introduces a general description of other aggravated felonies and does not expand the scope of the offense.[63] She then highlights the consequences of an expansive reading, which could include low-level offenses that are not "especially egregious felonies" as aggravated felonies, leading to arbitrary enforcement.[64]

Fourth, Justice Sotomayor argues that in deportation cases, any lingering ambiguities should be resolved in favor of the noncitizen.[65] She emphasizes that deportation is a drastic and harsh measure.[66] She argues that the Court should narrowly interpret the statute to protect noncitizens' freedom.[67] Justice Sotomayor asserts that given the high stakes involved, "[t]he Court should have 'erred on the side of underinclusiveness'" and not assume that Congress intended to encroach on the freedom of non-U.S. citizens beyond what is required by the narrowest interpretation of the words used.[68]

Fifth and finally, Justice Sotomayor argues that the Court's decision to reject the requirement of a pending investigation or proceeding for obstruction of justice opens the door for the government to use the provision as a catchall for various criminal activities.[69] She criticizes the Court for not providing clear boundaries to the concept of obstruction of justice, failing to define it in any meaningful way.[70] She challenges the Court's premise that dissuading a witness from reporting a crime qualifies as obstruction of justice, stating that Congress has not specifically included witness tampering as an aggravated felony in the Immigration and Nationality Act.[71] She asserts that the Court's decision encroaches on Congress's role and engages in judicial policymaking.[72] Justice Sotomayor urges lower courts to exercise caution when faced with questions about other offenses' qualifications under the provision and emphasizes the need for further analysis and clarity in future cases.[73]

Santos-Zacaria v. Garland[74]

Estrella Santos-Zacaria is a transgender Guatemalan woman involved in removal proceedings.[75] Santos-Zacaria left Guatemala in her teens to avoid physical harm and death threats because of her gender.[76] Santos-Zacaria briefly took shelter in the United States until immigration authorities removed her in 2008.[77] She returned to the country in 2018, and immigration authorities apprehended her again.[78] She challenged her deportation, citing transphobic persecution in her home country.[79] Still, the immigration judge denied her request for protection from deportation. Santos-Zacaria appealed to the Board of Immigration Appeals (BIA).[80] The BIA upheld the immigration judge's ruling.[81] Santos-Zacaria filed a petition for review in the Court of Appeals for the Fifth Circuit, citing U.S.C. § 1252 and claiming that the Board had unlawfully conducted factfinding that the immigration judge should have performed.[82] The Fifth Circuit, in a 2–1 decision, dismissed her claim, holding that Santos-Zacaria had not met

§ 1252(d)(1)'s exhaustion requirement, which the court raised *sua sponte.*[83] Section 1252(d)(1) states, "A court may review a final order of removal only if . . . the [non-citizen] has exhausted all administrative remedies available to the [noncitizen] as of right."[84] The Fifth Circuit interpreted § 1252(d)(1) as jurisdictional.[85] It concluded that Santos-Zacaria had not met the exhaustion requirement because she had not raised her impermissible-factfinding claim before filing her request for judicial review.[86]

The Supreme Court granted review on two important issues in immigration law. First, "whether § 1252(d)(1)'s exhaustion requirement is jurisdictional," and second, "whether § 1252(d)(1) requires seeking discretionary administrative review, like reconsideration by the Board of Immigration Appeals."[87]

The Court was unanimous in reversing the Fifth Circuit, with Justice Jackson writing for the Court, and Justices Alito and Thomas concurring in the judgment. As for the first issue, the Court followed a recent trend in putting a strong presumption against finding a statute is jurisdictional.[88] The Court has said that because of the severity of jurisdictional rules, it follows a clear-statement principle: a rule is treated as jurisdictional "only if Congress 'clearly states' that it is."[89] The Court concluded that § 1252(d)(1) fails this clear-statement principle.[90]

As for the second issue, the Supreme Court held § 1252(d)(1) "requires exhausting only remedies available 'as of right,' it does not require exhausting discretionary review."[91] Justice Jackson explained that § 1252(d)(1) demands exhausting only remedies "available . . . as of right," which is "a familiar phrase in the law, meaning '[b]y virtue of a legal entitlement.'"[92] Reconsideration by the Board is discretionary and therefore not "as of right."[93]

Justice Alito agreed with the majority that 8 U.S.C. § 1252(d)(1) does not mandate filing a motion for reconsideration. He adds that the provision requires only exhaustion of remedies "available to [a noncitizen] as of right," and the decision to grant reconsideration is discretionary. The divergence from the Court is when he says, "Because that determination disposes of the case, I would not decide whether § 1252(d)(1) is jurisdictional with respect to the administrative remedies to which it does apply."[94]

Endnotes

1. 143 S. Ct. at 1964 (2023).
2. 143 S. Ct. 1932 (2023).
3. 8 U.S.C. § 1324(a)(1)(A)(iv).
4. 143 S. Ct. 1932 at 1937.
5. *Id.* at 1938.
6. *Id.* at 1938.
7. *Id.* at 1937 (quoting United States v. Williams, 553 U.S. 285, 292 (2008)).
8. *Id.* at 1940 (citing Model Penal Code § 5.02(1) (Am. Law Inst. 1985); LaFave Substantive Criminal Law § 11.1 (3d ed. 2022); *see e.g., Twitter, Inc. v. Taamneh*, 143 S. Ct. 1206, 1221-1222 (2023)).
9. *Id.* at 1940–41.
10. *Id.* at 1941.
11. *Id.* at 1944.
12. *Id.* at 1944.
13. *Id.* at 1946.
14. *Id.* at 1947.
15. *Id.* at 1953 (Jackson, J., dissenting).
16. *Id.* (Jackson, J., dissenting) (quoting United States v. Stevens, 559 U.S. 460, 473 (2010)).
17. *Id.* at 1954 (Jackson, J., dissenting).
18. *Id.*
19. *Id.* at 1954–56 (Jackson, J., dissenting).
20. *Id.* at 1955 (Jackson, J., dissenting).
21. *Id.* at 1956 (Jackson, J., dissenting).
22. *Id.* at 1956–57 (Jackson, J., dissenting).
23. *Id.* at 1962–64 (Jackson, J., dissenting).
24. 143 S. Ct. 1833 (2023).
25. *Id.* at 1838.
26. *Id.*
27. *See* 8 U.S.C. §§ 1101(a)(43)(S), 1227(a)(2)(A)(iii).
28. 143 S. Ct. 1833 at 1838.
29. *Id.*
30. *Id.*
31. *Pugin v. Garland*, 19 F.4th 437 (4th Cir. 2021), *cert. granted in part*, 143 S. Ct. 645, *aff'd*, 143 S. Ct. 1833 (2023). *Cordero-Garcia v. Garland*, 44 F.4th 1181 (9th Cir. 2022), *cert. granted in part*, 143 S. Ct. 644 (2023), and *rev'd and remanded sub nom. Pugin v. Garland*, 143 S. Ct. 1833 (2023).
32. 143 S. Ct. 1833 at 1838.

33. *Id.* at 1838.
34. *Id.*
35. *Id.* at 1839.
36. 8 U.S.C. § 1227(a)(2)(A)(iii).
37. *See* § 1101(a)(43).
38. *See* § 1101(a)(43)(S).
39. 143 S. Ct. 1833 at 1839 (*citing Esquivel-Quintana v. Sessions*, 581 U.S. 385, 389 (2017); Moncrieffe v. Holder, 569 U.S. 184, 190 (2013)).
40. *Id.* (*citing Taylor v. United States*, 495 U.S. 575, 601 (1990)).
41. *Id.* at 1839.
42. *Id.*
43. *Id.* (citing MERRIAM-WEBSTER'S DICTIONARY OF LAW 337 (1996); B. GARNER, A DICTIONARY OF MODERN LEGAL USAGE 611 (2d ed. 1995); BLACK'S LAW DICTIONARY 1077 (6th ed. 1990); *cf.* Esquivel-Quintana v. Sessions, 581 U.S. 385, 391-92 (2017)).
44. *Id.*
45. *Id.* at 1840 (citing MODEL PENAL CODE § 240.0(4) (AM. LAW INST. 1980).
46. *Id.* at 1840.
47. *Id.* at 1841.
48. *Id.*
49. *Id.* (*citing Coventry Health Care of Missouri, Inc. v. Nevils*, 581 U.S. 87, 96 (2017)).
50. *Id.*
51. *See e.g., Shaw v. United States*, 580 U.S. 63, 71, (2016); *Salman v. United States*, 580 U.S. 39, 51, (2016); *Abramski v. United States*, 573 U.S. 169, 188, n. 10 (2014); *cf. Kawashima v. Holder*, 565 U.S. 478, 489 (2012).
52. 143 S. Ct. 1833 at 1846 (Sotomayor, J., dissenting).
53. *Id.*
54. *Id.*
55. *Id.*
56. *Id.* at 1847 (Sotomayor, J., dissenting).
57. *Id.*
58. *Id.* at 1848 (Sotomayor, J., dissenting).
59. *Id.* at 1853 (Sotomayor, J., dissenting).
60. *Id.* at 1853–54 (Sotomayor, J., dissenting).
61. *Id.*
62. *Id.*
63. *Id.*
64. *Id.* at 1854 (Sotomayor, J., dissenting).
65. *Id.*

66. *Id.* (*citing Fong Haw Tan v. Phelan*, 333 U.S. 6, 10 (1948) and *Carachuri-Rosendo v. Holder*, 560 U.S. 563, 566 (2010)).
67. *Id.* at 1855 (Sotomayor, J., dissenting).
68. *Id.* at 1856 (Sotomayor, J., dissenting).
69. *Id.*
70. *Id.*
71. *Id.*
72. *Id.* (*quoting Perieda v. Wilkinson*, 141 S. Ct. 754, 767 (2021)).
73. *Id.* (Sotomayor, J., dissenting).
74. 143 S. Ct. 1103 (2023).
75. *Id.* at 1110.
76. *Id.*
77. *Id.*
78. *Id.*
79. *Id.*
80. *Id.* at 1110–11.
81. *Id.* at 1111.
82. *Id.*
83. *Id.*
84. *Id.*
85. *Id.*
86. *Id.*
87. *Id.* at 1111.
88. *Id.* at 1111–12 (*quoting Kontrick v. Ryan*, 540 U.S. 443, 455 (2004)).
89. *Id.* at 1112.
90. *Id.*
91. *Id.* at 1117.
92. *Id.* at 1116–17 (*citing* Black's Law Dictionary 141 (11th ed. 2019)).
93. *Id.* at 1117.
94. *Id.* at 1120 (Alito, J., concurring).

11

Indian Law

The Court decided two important cases concerning Native Americans. They were in very different areas of law. In *Haaland v. Brackeen*, the Court upheld the constitutionality of the Indian Child Welfare Act, but left unresolved important constitutional questions regarding the law.[1] In *Arizona v. Navajo Nation*, the Court ruled that the Treaty of 1868 with the Navajo Nation does not require the United States to take affirmative steps to secure water rights for the tribal nation.[2]

Haaland v. Brackeen

The United States has a long and despicable history of removing Native American children from their families. As Justice Neil Gorsuch observed, there was "mass removal of Indian children from their families during the 1950s, 1960s, and 1970s by state officials and private parties."[3] This horrific practice actually began 150 years ago. Congress, in 1978, lamented that "an alarmingly high percentage of Indian families are broken up by the removal, often unwarranted, of their children from them by nontribal public and private agencies."[4]

In response, Congress adopted the Indian Child Welfare Act in 1978, which provides that preference should be given to Native American families when Native American children are placed in foster care or for adoption. As the Supreme Court noted, the "law requires a state court to place an Indian child with an Indian caretaker, if one is available. That is so even if the child is already living with a non-Indian family and the state court thinks it in the child's best interest to stay there."[5]

Several families challenged the constitutionality of the Indian Child Welfare Act in federal court. The named plaintiffs in the case were the Brackeens. A child referred to as "A.L.M." was placed in foster care with Chad and Jennifer Brackeen when he was 10 months old. The Brackeens sought to adopt him after he had lived with them for more than a year. A.L.M.'s parents are both Native American: His mother is a member of the Navajo Nation and his father is a member of the Cherokee Nation. Both of these biological parents supported having the Brackeens adopt A.L.M. But the Navajo and Cherokee Nations did not support this adoption. The Navajo Nation said that it had an alternative placement for the child with nonrelative tribal members living in New Mexico. Under the Indian Child Welfare Act, the child would be placed with the proposed Navajo family.

The Brackeens, and other families, filed suit in federal court against the United States, the Department of the Interior and its Secretary (Debra Haaland), the Bureau of Indian Affairs (BIA) and its Director, and the Department of Health and Human Services and its Secretary. The Brackeens challenged the constitutionality of this law and Texas intervened to do the same, while several Native American tribes intervened to defend it.

The federal district court declared the Indian Child Welfare Act unconstitutional. The United States Court of Appeals for the Fifth Circuit, in an *en banc* decision, affirmed this conclusion, though it did not agree with all of the lower court's analysis.

In *Haaland v. Brackeen*, the Supreme Court upheld the constitutionality of the Indian Child Welfare Act. It was a 7–2 decision, with Justice Amy Coney Barrett writing the opinion for the Court and only Justices Clarence Thomas and Samuel Alito dissenting. The Court was emphatic in upholding the law. The Court declared: "[T]he bottom line is that we reject all of petitioners' challenges to the statute, some on the merits and others for lack of standing."[6] But it also should be noted that one of the most difficult issues in the case—whether the statute is an impermissible racial preference—was not resolved and will surely be addressed by the Court in the future.

The Supreme Court considered several constitutional challenges to the Indian Child Welfare Act. First, the Court rejected the argument that the statute exceeded the scope of Congress's powers under Article I of the Constitution. The Constitution gives Congress the authority "[t]o regulate Commerce . . . with the Indian Tribes."[7] This has been interpreted to mean not just a power to regulate trade but also broad authority to legislate as to Indian affairs. Additionally, the federal government has the power to make treaties with Indian tribes, and the structure of the Constitution has been interpreted as reinforcing expansive federal powers in this area.

The Court noted that it had long "characterized Congress's power to legislate with respect to the Indian tribes as 'plenary and exclusive.'"[8] Likewise, "Congress's power to legislate with respect to Indians is well established and broad."[9] Although Congress's authority is not unlimited, the Court found that the Indian Child Welfare Act fit within Congress's powers to legislate as to Indian affairs.

Second, the Court rejected the argument that the Indian Child Welfare Act was impermissible "commandeering" of state governments in violation of the Tenth Amendment. The Supreme Court—in cases such as *New York v. United States* (1992),[10] *Printz v. United States* (1997),[11] and *Murphy v. NCAA* (2018)[12]—held that Congress cannot compel state governments to enact laws or regulations or to administer federal mandates. The challengers argued that the Indian Child Welfare Act impermissibly commandeered state courts to follow detailed procedures when considering the placement of a Native American child, to give preference to Native American families, and to maintain and transmit to the federal government detailed records.

The Court rejected these arguments that the Act violated the Tenth Amendment. It stressed that the law applies whether a foster placement or an adoption is privately initiated or state-initiated, writing that "[l]egislation that applies 'evenhandedly' to state and private actors does not typically implicate the Tenth Amendment."[13] Most importantly, the Court emphasized that where Congress has the authority to legislate it can prescribe legal standards that preempt state law and must be followed by state courts. This is what Congress did in the Indian Child Welfare

Act in requiring that a preference be given for Native American families when Native American children are placed in foster care or for adoption. It is not impermissible commandeering to require that state courts apply federal law. Nor is it unconstitutional, the Court said, for Congress to compel state courts to keep records in these cases and to provide them to the federal government.

The Court's reasoning in upholding the Indian Child Welfare Act will have important implications for other matters as well. If the Court had narrowly interpreted Congress's power to legislate as to Indian affairs, say by limiting it to regulating trade, many other federal statutes in this area would have been constitutionally vulnerable. If the Court had ruled that Congress cannot force state courts to apply federal law, the implications would have been huge.

There were two other legal challenges to the Indian Child Welfare Act that the Court did not resolve, instead dismissing them on standing grounds. One claim is that the Act establishes an unconstitutional racial preference by requiring a preference for Native Americans over non-Native Americans in placing children in foster care and for adoption. The other argument was that the statute impermissibly delegates federal legislative power to Indian tribes.

The Court said that neither the individual plaintiffs nor the State of Texas had standing to raise these claims. The Court explained that no relief that could be granted against the defendants—federal officials and federal agencies—could remedy these harms. The Court said that "Texas also lacks standing to challenge the placement preferences [because it] has no equal protection rights of its own."[14]

The equal protection claim is very likely to arise in the future and ultimately need to be resolved by the Supreme Court. Justice Brett Kavanaugh wrote a concurring opinion to express the view that "the equal protection issue is serious" as it will ultimately determine the constitutionality of the law.[15] The underlying question is whether a preference for Native Americans should be regarded as a racial preference, as Justice Kavanaugh asserts, or as a preference based on political status because Native American tribes are sovereign entities.

If the Court ultimately decides that this is a racial preference, then the Act is unlikely to be upheld by a Court that has expressed great hostility to racial preferences. It also then would endanger many programs, including scholarship programs, that provide benefits to Native Americans. But if this is seen as a preference based on political status, it is far more likely to be upheld.

Justice Gorusch also wrote a concurring opinion, joined by Justices Sotomayor and Kagan, in which he recited the long history of abusive practices toward Native Americans, including in removing children from their homes and communities. He said, "[t]o appreciate fully the significance of today's decision requires an understanding of the long line of policies that drove Congress to adopt ICWA. And to appreciate why that law surely comports with the Constitution requires a bird's-eye view of how our founding document mediates between competing federal, state, and tribal claims of sovereignty."[16] He left no doubt that he believes that the Indian Child Welfare Act is both essential and constitutional.

The bottom line is that the decision is an important victory for the Indian Child Welfare Act. But the hardest issue—is it an unconstitutional racial preference—remains and is sure to return to the Supreme Court.

Arizona v. Navajo Nation

In a 5–4 decision, the Court held that the Treaty of 1868 with the Navajo Nation does not require the United States to take affirmative steps to secure water rights for the tribal nation because there was no affirmative requirement in the treaty's text or history.[17]

The Navajo Reservation spans over 17 million acres across Arizona, New Mexico, and Utah. The reservation was established in connection with two treaties that date back to the mid-1800s. The Treaty of 1868 specifies that the Navajo Reservation includes not only the land with the reservation's boundaries but also water rights. Under the Court's long-standing reserved water rights doctrine, also referred to as the *Winters* doctrine, the "Federal Government's reservation of land for an Indian tribe also implicitly reserves the right to use needed water from various sources—such as groundwater, rivers, streams, lakes, and springs—that arise on, border, cross, underlie, or are encompassed within the reservation."[18] Under the *Winters* doctrine, the Federal Government reserves water only "to the extent needed to accomplish the purpose of the reservation."[19]

The Navajo Reservation lies within the Colorado River Basin, and on its border are three vital rivers. Although the Navajos are near water sources, the Navajo face the same water scarcity problem as all in that part of the country.

Over the decades, the Federal Government has "secured hundreds of thousands of acre-feet of water and authorized billions of dollars for water infrastructure on the Navajo Reservation."[20] But the Navajo view the government's actions as insufficient and a "breach of trust." The Navajo sued multiple federal agencies to "compel the Federal Defendants to determine the water required to meet the needs" of the Navajos in Arizona and to "devise a plan to meet those needs."[21] The Navajo argue that, instead of "simply not interfer[ing] with the reserved water right," the United States must "take affirmative steps to secure water for the Tribe—for example, by assessing the Tribe's water needs, developing a plan to secure the needed water, and potentially building pipelines, pumps, wells, or other water infrastructure."[22]

The U.S. District Court for the District of Arizona dismissed the Navajo's case because the court determined that the 1868 treaty did not impose a duty on the United States to take affirmative steps to secure water for the Tribe. The Navajo appealed, and the Ninth Circuit reversed, holding "that the United States has a duty under the 1868 treaty to take affirmative steps to secure water for the Navajos."[23]

The Supreme Court reversed the Ninth Circuit in an opinion by Justice Kavanaugh. Justice Gorsuch wrote a vehement dissent, joined by Justices Sotomayor, Kagan, and Jackson.

The Court said that for a tribe to win a "breach of trust claim," a Tribe "must establish, among other things, that the text of a treaty, statute, or regulation imposed certain duties on the United States."[24] Additionally, the Court stated that the Federal Government "owes judicially enforceable duties to a tribe 'only to the extent it expressly accepts those responsibilities.'"[25] Furthermore, the Court clarified that an "expressly accepted" obligation "must train on specific rights-creating or duty-imposing" language in a treaty, statute, or regulation."[26] The Court stated that these requirements stem from the separation of powers principles; the relationship between the United States and Native American tribes is left to the President and Congress. As a result, "the federal courts, in turn, must adhere to the text of the relevant law—here the treaty."[27]

The Court explained that what the 1868 treaty did instead was "set apart" a reservation for the "use and occupation of the Navajo tribe." The Court said that the treaty contained no "rights-creating or duty-imposing" language that "imposed a duty on the United States" to "take affirmative steps to secure water for the Tribe."[28] The Court acknowledged that the treaty did impose many duties on the United States, encompassing tasks like constructing certain buildings, providing clothes, and helping with agriculture tasks. But the Court said that an "affirmative duty" to secure water is missing from the treaty. Justifying its holding, the Court explained that "Indian treaties cannot be rewritten or expanded beyond their clear terms."[29] The Court's focus was on the plain language of the treaty, and it did not find within that a commitment of the United States to protect the water rights of the Native American tribe.

Justice Gorsuch wrote a strong dissent joined by Justices Sotomayor, Kagan, and Jackson. As in *Brackeen*—and the recent decisions in *McGirt v. Oklahoma*[30] and *Castro-Huerta v. Oklahoma*[31]—Justice Gorsuch staunchly defended Native American rights and sovereignty. He wrote: "the Navajo have a simple ask: They want the United States to identify the water rights it holds for them. And if the United States has misappropriated the Navajo's water rights, the Tribe asks it to formulate a plan to stop doing so prospectively. Because there is nothing remarkable about any of this, I would allow the Navajo's case to proceed."[32] He provided a detailed description of the history of the United States relationship with the Navajos, especially with regard to water rights.

He lamented the Court's decision but said that the Navajo still could intervene in the ongoing litigation concerning allocation of water in the Colorado River. He concluded: "All of which leaves the Navajo in a familiar spot. As they did at Bosque Redondo, they must again fight for themselves to secure their homeland and all that must necessarily come with it. Perhaps here, as there, some measure of justice will prevail in the end."[33]

Although this case was about the important issue of water, the larger underlying issue is how treaties with Indian tribes should be interpreted. On that, the case reveals a sharp difference among the justices.

Endnotes

1. 143 S. Ct. 1609 (2023).
2. 143 S. Ct. 1804 (2023).
3. 143 S. Ct. at 1641 (Gorsuch, J., concurring).
4. *Id.* at 1646.
5. 143 S. Ct. at 1622.
6. *Id.* at 1623.
7. U.S. CONST. art. I, § 8, cl. 3.
8. 143 S. Ct. 1609 at 1627.
9. *Id.* at 1628.
10. 505 U.S. 144 (1992).
11. 521 U.S. 898 (1997)
12. 138 S. Ct. 1461 (2018).
13. 143 S. Ct. 1609 at 1633.
14. *Id.* at 1640.
15. *Id.* at 1661 (Kavanaugh, J., concurring).
16. *Id.* at 1641 (Gorsuch, J., concurring).
17. 143 S. Ct. 1804 at 1809.
18. *Id.* at 1811; *see Winters v. United States*, 207 U.S. 564, 576–77 (1908).
19. *Id.* at 1811.
20. *Id.* at 1811–12.
21. *Id.* at 1812.
22. *Id.*
23. *Id.*
24. *Id.* at 1813; *see United States v. Jicarilla Apache Nation*, 564 U.S. 162, 173–74 (2011)
25. 143 S. Ct. 1804 at 1813.
26. *Id.*; *see United States* v. *Navajo Nation*, 537 U.S. 488, 506 (2003).
27. 143 S. Ct. 1804 at 1813.
28. *Id.*
29. *Id* (quoting Choctaw Nation v. United States, 318 U.S. 423, 432 (1943)).
30. 140 S. Ct. 2452 (2020).
31. 142 S. Ct. 2486 (2022).
32. 143 S. Ct. 1804 at 1819 (Gorsuch, J., dissenting).
33. *Id.* at 1833.

12

Intellectual Property

There were a number of important intellectual property cases from the term. The Court consistently ruled in favor of intellectual property rights. The context of the most prominent cases varied between copyright and trademark, but the ultimate outcome was the same, with the Court ruling in favor of those who asserted claims under intellectual property laws.

Andy Warhol Foundation for the Visual Arts v. Goldsmith

The intellectual property case that received the most media attention was *Andy Warhol Foundation for the Visual Arts v. Goldsmith*,[1] which dealt with what constitutes "fair use" within the Copyright Act. A copyright owner is guaranteed the exclusive right to create adaptations and derivatives of their copyrighted work. But if a use that might potentially infringe is sufficiently "transformative," then it is likely to be deemed fair use—that is, noninfringing. This case attempts to draw the line, in the visual arts context, for when an adaption of a copyrighted work is "derivative" and when it is "transformative."

In 1981, *Newsweek* commissioned Lynn Goldsmith, a renowned professional photographer, to take a photo of a then up-and-coming musician named Prince Rogers Nelson. *Newsweek* published the photo, along with an article about Prince.

In 1984, Goldsmith, through her agency, licensed that photograph to *Vanity Fair* to serve as an "artist reference for an illustration" in the magazine. The terms of the license were that the illustration was "to be published in *Vanity Fair* November 1984 issue. It can appear one time full page and one time under one quarter page. No other usage right granted."[2] Goldsmith was to receive $400 and a source credit.

To make the illustration, *Vanity Fair* hired famous artist Andy Warhol. Warhol used Goldsmith's photo to create a silkscreen portrait of Prince, which, as planned, appeared alongside an article about Prince in the November 1984 issue of *Vanity Fair.* Goldsmith received her $400 fee and *Vanity Fair* credited her for the "source photograph."

After Prince died in 2016, *Vanity Fair*'s parent company, Condé Nast, asked the Andy Warhol Foundation about reusing the 1984 *Vanity Fair* image for a special edition magazine that would commemorate Prince. Condé Nast then learned that Warhol had used this silkscreen to create 15 other images, the Prince Series. Condé Nast paid the Andy Warhol Foundation $10,000 for a license to use one of these Prince pieces—"Orange Prince"—in a magazine story. Although Goldsmith was credited and paid by *Vanity Fair* for the first publication, she received no compensation for this subsequent use by Condé Nast.

The issue was whether the Andy Warhol Foundation's subsequent use of this photo for its financial benefit was "fair use" within the meaning of the copyright law. The Supreme Court, in an opinion by Justice Sotomayor, found that it was not fair use. The decision was 7–2 with Justice Kagan, joined by Chief Justice Roberts, strongly dissenting.

The question of whether there is "fair use" is critical in many cases in determining whether there has been a copyright infringement. Section 107 of the Copyright Act identifies four nonexclusive factors to be considered in determining whether there is fair use:

> "(1) the purpose and character of the use, including whether such use is of a commercial nature or is for nonprofit educational purposes;

(2) the nature of the copyrighted work;
(3) the amount and substantiality of the portion used in relation to the copyrighted work as a whole; and
(4) the effect of the use upon the potential market for or value of the copyrighted work."[3]

The Court in its analysis focused solely on the first factor. The Andy Warhol Foundation argued that its use was "transformative" based on how much Warhol's creativity transformed the original Goldsmith photograph and thus should be deemed fair use.

But the Court disagreed. It held that Andy Warhol's use wasn't transformative enough to tilt the first fair use factor—which it said focuses primarily on the purposes of the uses and whether they were sufficiently different—in Warhol's favor. Justice Sotomayor wrote that "the first fair use factor instead focuses on whether an allegedly infringing use has a further purpose or different character, which is a matter of degree, and the degree of difference must be weighed against other considerations, like commercialism."[4]

Although Warhol added new content through his silk screen, the Court noted that "the original photograph and [Andy Warhol Foundation's] copying use of it share substantially the same purpose. Moreover, the copying use is of a commercial nature."[5] The Court explained that fair use is ultimately a balancing test that weighs the benefits of incentives to create against the costs of restrictions on copying. The Court stated the "central" question it asks is "whether the new work merely 'supersede[s] the objects' of the original creation . . . ('supplanting' the original), or instead adds something new, with a further purpose or different character."[6]

The Court used a critical book review as an example to highlight how a piece can be "manifestly different" and not just a "copy" or "substitute" that merely supplants an original work. Although the review may quote passages from the book, the quotes will "likely serve a different purpose." The Court cautioned that adding something new "alone" does not render the use fair because the first factor asks "whether and to what extent" the use at issue has a "purpose or character" different from the original.[7] The

Court succinctly summarized the test: "the first fair use factor considers whether the use of a copyrighted work has a further purpose or different character, which is a matter of degree, and the degree of difference must be balanced against the commercial nature of the use. If an original work and a secondary use share the same or highly similar purposes, and the secondary use is of a commercial nature, the first factor is likely to weigh against fair use, absent some other justification for copying."[8]

The Court concluded that the purpose of the "Orange Prince" photo submitted to Condé Nast was substantially the same as that of Goldsmith's photograph. Both portraits of Prince are used in magazines to illustrate stories about Prince and that these "environments" are not "distinct and different."[9] Both uses were for commercial purpose. Thus, the Court said that the use of the photos did not meet the requirements for fair use under the first part of the test.

Justice Kagan's wrote a vehement dissent and focused on the transformative nature of Warhol's work and said that the majority erred by not making that decisive in the fair use analysis. She accused the majority of leaving analysis under the first fair use factor in "shambles."[10] Justice Kagan lamented the majority's emphasis on the purpose of the licensing rather than the extent to which Warhol changed the Goldsmith photo. She wrote: "It does not matter how different the Warhol is from the original photo—how much 'new expression, meaning, or message' he added. It does not matter that the silkscreen and the photo do not have the same aesthetic characteristics and do not convey the same meaning. It does not matter that because of those dissimilarities, the magazine publisher did not view the one as a substitute for the other. All that matters is that Warhol and the publisher entered into a licensing transaction, similar to one Goldsmith might have done. Because the artist had such a commercial purpose, all the creativity in the world could not save him."[11]

Justice Kagan said that the focus should be on the creativity of the work and how much it changed the original, not whether it is commercially used for the same purpose as the earlier license. She powerfully concluded her dissent by criticizing the impact of the majority's decision: "It will stifle creativity of every sort. It will impede new art and music and literature. It will thwart the expression of new ideas and the attainment of new knowledge. It will make our world poorer."[12]

The case is significant because it is the first full case in which the court has considered fair use—one of the most significant defenses to copyright infringement—and transformativeness in the context of visual art. It also reflects very different views between the majority and the dissent as to how the balancing should be done in determining fair use. For Justice Sotomayor and the majority, the focus is on whether the photo was commercially used for the same purpose for which it was licensed. For Justice Kagan, the focus is on the degree of creativity involved.

Jack Daniel's Properties, Inc. v. VIP Products LLC

One of the most fun cases of the term is *Jack Daniel's Properties, Inc. v. VIP Products LLC.*[13] VIP Products LLC is a company that makes dog toys designed to resemble everyday products. It made a dog toy designed to look like a bottle of Jack Daniel's. Instead of the traditional labeling on the bottle of whiskey, it featured puns and jokes. For example, "the words 'Jack Daniel's' become 'Bad Spaniels' and the descriptive phrase 'Old No. 7 Brand Tennessee Sour Mash Whiskey' turns into 'The Old No. 2 On Your Tennessee Carpet.'"[14]

Jack Daniel's Properties owns the trademarks to the "distinctive" Jack Daniel's bottle, which VIP Products parodied with the "Bad Spaniels" toy. Soon after the Bad Spaniels toy hit the market, Jack Daniel's demanded that VIP stop selling it. VIP filed suit, seeking a declaratory judgment that Bad Spaniels neither infringed nor diluted Jack Daniel's trademarks. Jack Daniel's counterclaimed for infringement and dilution.

The Court unanimously ruled in favor of Jack Daniels, with Justice Kagan writing the opinion and with separate concurring opinions by Justices Sotomayor and Gorsuch. Justice Kagan began by stressing the reasons why the law protects trademark registrations. She wrote: "[T]rademarks benefit consumers and producers alike. A source-identifying mark enables customers to select 'the goods and services that they wish to purchase, as well as those they want to avoid.' The mark 'quickly and easily assures a potential customer that *this* item—the item with this mark—is made by the same producer as other similarly marked items that he or she liked (or disliked) in the past.'"[15]

Justice Kagan explained that the Lanham Act, which protects trademarks, creates a cause of action both for "infringement" of the trademark and for "dilution." She noted that in the typical case of infringement, "the owner of a mark sues someone using a mark that closely resembles its own. The court must decide whether the defendant's use is 'likely to cause confusion, or to cause mistake, or to deceive.'"[16] Often this comes down to confusion about the source of a product or service. A cause of action for dilution, by contrast, can occur without likelihood of confusion but when there is tarnishment that can "harm[ ] the reputation of the famous mark."[17]

As for infringement, the primary question before the Court was whether to apply a test developed by the Second Circuit in *Rogers v. Grimaldi* to protect artistic expression.[18] Under it, dismissal of an infringement claim at the outset is appropriate unless the complainant can show one of two things: that the challenged use of a mark "has no artistic relevance to the underlying work" or that it "explicitly misleads as to the source or the content of the work."[19]

The Supreme Court ruled that the *Rogers* test did not apply in this context but left open the question of whether it can be used in other types of trademark infringement claims. Justice Kagan wrote: "Without deciding whether *Rogers* has merit in other contexts, we hold that it does not when an alleged infringer uses a trademark in the way the Lanham Act most cares about: as a designation of source for the infringer's own goods. VIP used the marks derived from Jack Daniel's in that way, so the infringement claim here rises or falls on likelihood of confusion."[20] Justice Kagan explained: "The point is that whatever you make of *Rogers*—and again, we take no position on that issue—it has always been a cabined doctrine. If we put this case to the side, the *Rogers* test has applied only to cases involving 'non-trademark uses'—or otherwise said, cases in which 'the defendant has used the mark' at issue in a 'non-source-identifying way.' The test has not insulated from ordinary trademark scrutiny the use of trademarks as trademarks, 'to identify or brand [a defendant's] goods or services.'"[21]

Justice Kagan does three things here. First, she expressly declines to decide whether *Rogers* is good law. Second, she holds that *Rogers* does not apply when a trademark defendant uses their mark "as a designation of source for" their goods. (In other words, when they use the plaintiff's trademark as a trademark.) VIP obviously used its infringing mark as a mark—it even registered it with the US Patent Trademark Office. Third, she says that, even without First Amendment protection, a parody may nevertheless not infringe if consumers would not be confused.

The Court remanded the case on the infringement issue, leaving the lower courts to answer the question of whether there was a likelihood of confusion.

The Court found the issue of dilution to be easier. The Court of Appeal had rejected the dilution claim because the dog toy was a parody, but Justice Kagan said that is too broad and that there can still be liability for dilution when there is confusion about the source of the product. A parodic use might be less likely to confuse consumers precisely because consumers will realize that it is a parody.

Justice Kagan concluded her majority opinion by stressing the limited scope of the Court's holding: "Today's opinion is narrow. We do not decide whether the *Rogers* test is ever appropriate, or how far the 'noncommercial use' exclusion goes. On infringement, we hold only that *Rogers* does not apply when the challenged use of a mark is as a mark. On dilution, we hold only that the noncommercial exclusion does not shield parody or other commentary when its use of a mark is similarly source-identifying. It is no coincidence that both our holdings turn on whether the use of a mark is serving a source-designation function. The Lanham Act makes that fact crucial, in its effort to ensure that consumers can tell where goods come from."[22]

Justice Sotomayor, wrote a concurring opinion joined by Justice Alito, emphasizing the need for caution when relying on surveys to demonstrate consumer confusion over parodies.[23] She wrote: "When an alleged trademark infringement involves a parody, however, there is particular risk in giving uncritical or undue weight to surveys. Survey answers may reflect a mistaken belief among some survey respondents that all parodies require permission from the owner of the parodied mark. . . . Allowing such survey results to drive the infringement analysis would risk silencing a great many parodies, even ones that by other metrics are unlikely to result in the confusion about sourcing that is the core concern of the Lanham Act."[24]

Justice Gorsuch wrote a short concurring opinion, joined by Justices Thomas and Barrett, to stress that the Court had taken no position on the use of the *Rogers* test.[25] He said lower courts should use it "with care," noting that its basis in the law was unclear and had not been addressed by the Court. This suggests that there are likely votes on the Court to reject the *Rogers* test.

The case was remanded to determine if there had been a trademark infringement or dilution. Although narrow, the ruling preserved the bite of trademark law in cases involving parody.

Abitron Austria GmbH v. Hetronic International, Inc

A final intellectual property case involved the application of the presumption against extraterritorial application of federal laws to the trademark context. In a number of relatively recent cases, the Supreme Court has said that there is a presumption against applying federal laws to conduct that occurs outside of the United States.[26] In Abitron Austria GmbH v. Hetronic International, Inc., the Supreme Court applied this presumption against extraterritorial application of federal law and ruled that the Lanham Act's protections of trademarks extend only to claims where the infringing use in commerce is domestic.[27]

The case concerns a trademark dispute between a US company, Hetronic International, Inc., and a group of foreign companies collectively known as Abitron. Hetronic manufactures remote controls for construction equipment and owns several trademarks. Hetronic used Abitron to distribute its parts across Europe. This partnership lasted until Abitron "claimed ownership" of the rights to much of Hetronic's intellectual property.

Hetronic sued Abitron in the Western District of Oklahoma for trademark violations under two related provisions of the Lanham Act, both of which prohibit the unauthorized use in commerce of protected marks when that use is "likely to cause confusion." Abitron argued that this suit is an impermissible extraterritorial application of the Lanham Act. The District Court disagreed, and, eventually, a jury awarded Hetronic $96 million in damages. Additionally, the District Court entered a permanent injunction preventing Abitron from using Hetronic's marks "anywhere in the world." Abitron appealed, and the Tenth Circuit narrowed the scope of the injunction but otherwise affirmed the judgment. The Tenth Circuit concluded that the Lanham Act extends to "all of Abitron's foreign infringing conduct" because the "impacts within the United States were of a sufficient character and magnitude [to] give the United States a reasonably strong interest in the litigation."[28]

The Supreme Court reversed. Justice Alito, writing for the Court, looked at the two Lanham Act provisions and determined that they do not provide "a clear, affirmative indication" that they apply extraterritorially.[29] The Court reasoned that neither provision has an "express statement of extraterritorial application."[30] Justice Alito concluded his opinion: "In sum, we hold that [the provisions of the Lanham Act] are not extraterritorial and that the infringing 'use in commerce' of a trademark provides the dividing line between foreign and domestic applications of these provisions."

The Court's approach is consistent with how it has read other federal statutes, creating a strong presumption against their extraterritorial application.

Endnotes

1. 143 S. Ct. 1258 (2023).
2. *Id.* at 1267.
3. *Id.* at 1298.
4. *Id.* at 1273.
5. *Id.*
6. *Id.* at 1274 (citing *Campbell v. Acuff-Rose Music, Inc.*, 510 U. S. 569, 579 (1994)).
7. *Id.* at 1273.
8. *Id.* at 1277.
9. *Id.* at 1279.
10. *Id.* at 1292 (Kagan, J., dissenting).
11. *Id.*
12. *Id.* at 1312.
13. 143 S. Ct. 1578 (2023).
14. *Id.* at 1585.
15. *Id.* at 1583.
16. Id at 1584.

17. *Id.*

18. *Rogers v. Grimaldi*, 875 F.2d 994, 999 (C.A.2 1989).

19. *Id.*

20. 143 S. Ct. at 1587.

21. *Id.* at 1589–90.

22. *Id.* at 1592–93.

23. *Id.* at 1593 (Sotomayor, J., concurring).

24. *Id.*

25. *Id.* at 1594 (Gorsuch, J., concurring).

26. *See, e.g., Morrison v. Nat'l Australia Bank Ltd.*, 561 U.S. 247, 255 (2010); *Kiobel v. Royal Dutch Petroleum Co.*, 569 U.S. 108, 119 (2013).

27. 143 S. Ct. 2522 (2023).

28. *Id.* at 2527.

29. *Id.* at 2529.

30. *Id.* at 2534.

13

Labor Law

When can a union be held liable for the economic consequences of a strike? On the one hand, union members do not have the right to destroy an employer's property as part of a strike. No one contends that a strike entails a right to throw bricks through the employer's windows or set the workplace on fire. On the other hand, virtually all strikes impose costs. That is exactly why they are an effective and essential labor tool. If unions were liable for all the costs resulting from their strikes, no unions ever would be able to strike.

The legal issue arises as to whether the National Labor Relations Act, which protects the right of unions to strike, preempts state tort liability for the economic consequences of a strike. There is also the question of what the role of the National Labor Relations Board is in determining whether the right to strike is protected in a particular situation and the role it plays in courts adjudicating tort suits.

These issues were presented in *Glacier Northwest, Inc. v. International Brotherhood of Teamsters Local No. 174.*[1] The case involved a strike by cement truck drivers. They had picked up their trucks on the morning of the strike and had begun driving them to their job sites. When the drivers began the strike that morning, they returned the trucks to their employer and left the drums turning so the trucks would not be damaged. But because the employer had chosen not to exercise its right to hire replacement workers or use nonstriking workers to deliver and pour the concrete, the cement was ruined.

Glacier Northwest sued the union for damages for the loss of the concrete. The Washington state supreme court ruled in favor of the union, rejecting liability for the "claims related to the loss of its concrete product because that loss was incidental to a strike arguably protected by federal law." [2] The Washington court concluded that state tort liability was preempted by federal law.

But the Supreme Court reversed in an 8–1 decision, with Justice Amy Coney Barrett writing for the majority. The Court stressed that "[t]he drivers engaged in a sudden cessation of work that put Glacier's property in foreseeable and imminent danger."[3] The Court said that the drivers' action ruined the concrete and risked serious harm to the trucks. The Court found that the union could be held liable because it "failed to take reasonable precautions to protect against this foreseeable and imminent danger."[4] The Court gave no weight to the fact that the employees returned the trucks with the drums running to prevent permanent damage to the cement trucks.

The central issue before the Court was whether the National Labor Relations Act, which protects the right of employees to strike, precludes a state court from imposing liability on a union for the economic consequences of a strike.

In 1959, in *San Diego Building Trades Council v. Garmon*, the Supreme Court ruled that state court proceedings should be paused to allow the National Labor Relations Board to determine whether the union's conduct was, or was not, protected or prohibited by the National Labor Relations Act.[5]

This approach allows a federal agency, vested with authority by Congress and with its own expertise, to make the threshold determination of whether the strike is protected or prohibited by federal law. Indeed, the National Labor Relations Board is in the midst of a factual investigation to determine whether federal law protects the strike conducted by these cement workers.

But the Supreme Court did not follow the procedure of allowing the National Labor Relations Board to make the initial determination of whether the strike was protected by federal law. The Court decided the issue for itself, concluding, based on its view that perhaps not every driver did enough to ensure the cement would not harden, that the strike was not even arguably protected by federal law, even though the National Labor Relations Board is still investigating and deciding that issue. By concluding that the strike was not "arguably protected" under the NLRA, there was not preemption of tort liability under *Garmon.*

Justice Barrett's majority opinion stressed that the "Union failed to 'take reasonable precautions to protect' against this foreseeable and imminent danger."[6] Justice Barrett said that "[i]ndeed, far from taking reasonable precautions to mitigate foreseeable danger to Glacier's property, the Union executed the strike in a manner designed to compromise the safety of Glacier's trucks and destroy its concrete. Such conduct is not 'arguably protected' by the NLRA; on the contrary, it goes well beyond the NLRA's protections."[7]

The Court acknowledged prior cases where employers lost perishable products as a result of a strike—such as poultry, milk, and eggs—but liability for the union was rejected. Justice Barrett said that those cases are distinguishable: "The Union is swinging at a straw man. It casts this case as one involving nothing more than a foreseeable risk that the employer's perishable products would spoil. But given the lifespan of wet concrete, Glacier could not batch it until a truck was ready to take it. So by reporting for duty and pretending as if they would deliver the concrete, the drivers *prompted the creation* of the perishable product. Then, they waited to walk off the job until the concrete was mixed and poured in the trucks. In so doing, they not only destroyed the concrete but also put Glacier's trucks in harm's way. This case therefore involves much more than 'a work stoppage at a time when the loss of perishable products is foreseeable.'"[8]

This case is important because it articulates a test for when unions can be held liable for the economic consequences of a strike: when there is "a risk of foreseeable, aggravated, and imminent harm."[9] The Court saw a strike that led to the loss of a perishable good as not meeting this standard, but the truck drivers' endangering the trucks and causing the loss of cement met this standard.

Justice Thomas, joined by Justice Gorsuch, concurred in the judgment and made clear that he would reconsider the decision in *San Diego Build-*

ing Trades Council v. Garmon and the preemption of state tort liability by federal law.[10] He said: "the parties here have not asked us to reconsider *Garmon*, nor is it necessary to do so to resolve this case. Nonetheless, in an appropriate case, we should carefully reexamine whether the law supports *Garmon*'s 'unusual' pre-emption regime."[11]

Justice Alito, joined by Justices Thomas and Gorsuch, argued that this was a simple case. The union acted in a way to harm the employer's property. That, Justice Alito said, is not protected by the National Labor Relations Act: "Nothing more is needed to resolve this case. Glacier's complaint alleges that the Union and its members acted with the improper purpose to harm Glacier by causing [its] batched concrete to be destroyed."[12]

Justice Jackson was the sole dissenter. She said that Congress enacted the National Labor Relations Act in 1935 precisely to prevent courts from deciding in this ad hoc way, based on untested employer allegations, that strikes violate some law. She argued that in allowing the union to be held liable for the consequences of its strike, the Court deals a serious blow to the federally protected right of workers to strike. In protecting a right to strike under the National Labor Relations Board, Congress knew that strikes impose economic costs on employers. As Justice Jackson said in her dissent, "the threat of economic harm posed by the right to strike is a feature, not a bug, of the NLRA."[13] The threat of economic loss—to employers and to striking workers—is what causes the parties to negotiate a settlement. As she observed, "Unions leverage a strike's economic harm (or the threat of it) into bargaining power, and then wield that power to demand improvement of employees' wages and working conditions."[14]

She saw the Court's new rule—that unions can be held liable for "foreseeable and imminent danger" of economic harm—as contrary to past cases that held unions could not be held liable when their strikes caused loss of perishable goods, like poultry, milk, and cheese. The Court said those cases are different, but it failed to say why. The majority emphasized that the cement workers went on strike without giving notice to the employer and thus endangered the cement and the trucks. But the National Labor Relations Act provides that *only* healthcare workers must give advance notice of the day and time a strike will commence. In these circumstances, state courts are not to wait for a determination from the NLRB as to whether the strike is arguably protected by federal law.

It is unclear what the case is likely to mean in terms of the role of the National Labor Relations Board in determining whether a strike is arguably protected by federal law and for when there can be tort liability for the economic consequences of a strike. The Court's standard now is that there can be liability when there is "a risk of foreseeable, aggravated, and imminent harm."

But it is unclear how that will be applied. All strikes (and employer lockouts) pose a "foreseeable" danger of harm. The strike by graduate students at the University of California in 2022 meant that some students did not get their grades on time and that might have hurt their employment prospects. The writers' strike in Hollywood will lead to economic harm to studios, caterers, actors, and set builders. Lockouts in professional sports have resulted in the cancellation of games and losses to players, TV networks, and peanut vendors.

The question will be where the line will be drawn as to when unions can be sued for damages. A narrow reading of the decision, which is sure to be urged by unions, is that the cement workers' conduct was akin to throwing a brick through the employers' window. It was intentional destruction of property and therefore not protected by the National Labor Relations Act. A broad reading of this ruling, sure to be urged by management, is that this decision significantly expands the liability of unions when their strikes cause harm. Ultimately, the Court will need to decide in the future how to determine what is "a risk of foreseeable, aggravated, and imminent harm."

Endnotes

1. 143 S. Ct. 1404 (2023).
2. *Id.* at 1408.
3. *Id.* at 1413.
4. *Id.* at 1408.
5. 359 U.S. 236 (1959).
6. 143 S. Ct. at 1413.
7. *Id.* at 1414.

8. *Id.* at 1414–15.
9. *Id.* at 1416.
10. *Id.* at 1417.
11. *Id.* (Thomas, J., concurring in the judgment).
12. *Id.* at 1418 (Alito, J., concurring in the judgment).
13. *Id.* at 1428 (Jackson, J., dissenting).
14. *Id.*

14

Personal Jurisdiction

When is consent a sufficient basis for personal jurisdiction? Or more precisely, may a state condition doing business in the state on a company registering and thereby consenting to personal jurisdiction? In *Mallory v. Norfolk Southern Railway Co.*, the Supreme Court, in a 5–4 decision, upheld a state creating personal jurisdiction by such consent, but the narrow ruling left open many important questions for the future.[1]

The Context

The Court has long ruled that due process limits the ability to sue an out-of-state defendant without their consent.[2] In the landmark case of *International Shoe v. State of Washington*, the Supreme Court ruled that absent consent, an out-of-state defendant may be sued only if it has "minimum contacts with the forum state."[3]

Over time, the Court developed the concepts of general jurisdiction and specific jurisdiction as ways for finding minimum contacts. Although many cases involving personal jurisdiction were decided by the Court without invoking these concepts, the Court has increasingly focused on them and has held that personal jurisdiction exists if there is either general or specific jurisdiction.

Both general and specific jurisdiction have been narrowed greatly in recent years. It used to be that general jurisdiction could be found if the defendant, in the words of *International Shoe*, had "systematic and continuous contacts" with the state.[4] But in cases such as *Goodyear Dunlop Tires Operations, S. A. v. Brown* (2011)[5] and *Daimler AG v. Bauman* (2014),[6] the Court held that general jurisdiction only exists when a defendant is "essentially at home" in the state. An individual is subject to general jurisdiction in his or her state of domicile, and a corporation is "home" in the state where it is incorporated or has its principal place of business.

Specific jurisdiction exists where the defendant's contacts with the state give rise to the cause of action. In recent years, the Court has restricted this type of jurisdiction as well. For example, in *Walden v. Fiore* (2014), the Court stressed that it is not enough that the defendant's conduct would foreseeably cause injury in a state; there is not personal jurisdiction if the defendant did not have the requisite contacts with the state where the suit is brought.[7]

In the recent decision, *Bristol-Myers Squibb Co.* v. *Superior Court of Cal., San Francisco Cty.*, the Court refused to allow out-of-state plaintiffs to sue a drug company for harms they suffered.[8] Even though the out-of-state plaintiffs were part of a lawsuit brought by in-state plaintiffs, the out-of-state plaintiffs had suffered the same injury as the in-state plaintiffs, and the drug they were suing over was marketed and sold in California, the Court rejected the existence of personal jurisdiction in an 8–1 decision. There was not general jurisdiction because Bristol-Myers Squibb is not home in California as it is not incorporated and does not have its principal place of business in California. The Court said that for specific jurisdiction to exist, "there must be 'an affiliation between the forum and the underlying controversy, principally, [an] activity or an occurrence that takes place in the forum State and is therefore subject to the State's regulation.'"[9] The Court stressed that personal jurisdiction is not only about fairness to the defendant; it is also about the constitutional limits on the reach of a state's territorial authority.

Consent as Alternative Way to Find Personal Jurisdiction

It has always been thought that consent is an alternative path to personal jurisdiction when there are not minimum contacts.[10] *Mallory v. Norfolk Southern Railway Co.* is about consent as a basis for personal jurisdiction in a particular context: when a state law conditions doing business in a state on consent to being sued in that state.

Robert Mallory worked for Norfolk Southern as a freight-car mechanic for nearly 20 years, first in Ohio, then in Virginia. He alleged that while working for the company, he was responsible for spraying boxcar pipes with asbestos and handling chemicals in the railroad's paint shop. He also demolished car interiors that, he alleges, contained carcinogens.

After his retirement, he developed colon cancer and believed it was caused by the chemicals he had been exposed to while working for Norfolk Southern Railway. He sued the company in Pennsylvania state court. He sued in Pennsylvania because he had lived there after retiring, and because Norfolk Southern Railway has extensive operations in the state. Pennsylvania law requires that out-of-state companies register to do business in the state and deems that such registration is consent to personal jurisdiction. The Supreme Court granted certiorari to decide "whether the Due Process Clause of the Fourteenth Amendment prohibits a State from requiring an out-of-state corporation to consent to personal jurisdiction to do business there."[11]

The Court ruled in favor of Mallory and allowed such consent as a basis for personal jurisdiction, with an unusual split among the justices. Justice Gorsuch wrote for the Court and was joined by Justices Thomas, Alito, Sotomayor, and Jackson. Justice Alito wrote an enigmatic concurring opinion that could matter greatly in the future. Justice Barrett wrote the dissent, joined by Chief Justice Roberts and Justices Kagan and Kavanaugh.

Justice Gorsuch's majority opinion saw the case as being resolved by a 1917 decision, *Pennsylvania Fire Ins. Co. of Philadelphia v. Gold Issue Mining & Milling Co.*,[12] where the Court "unanimously held that laws like Pennsylvania's comport with the Due Process Clause."[13] Justice Gorsuch's opinion declared: "*Pennsylvania Fire* controls this case. Much like the Missouri law at issue there, the Pennsylvania law at issue here provides that an out-of-state corporation 'may not do business in this Commonwealth until it registers with' the Department of State. . . . Among other things, Pennsylvania law is explicit that 'qualification as a foreign corporation' shall permit state courts to 'exercise general personal jurisdiction' over a registered foreign corporation, just as they can over domestic corporations."[14]

The Court expressly declined to overrule *Pennsylvania Fire*. Nor would it hold, as urged by Norfolk Railway, that there is only personal jurisdiction if either general or specific jurisdiction is present. The Court said that there was nothing unfair about Norfolk Railway being sued in Pennsylvania given its extensive contacts with the state. To be clear, the Court did not find that those contacts were sufficient for personal jurisdiction, as it might have when systematic and continuous contacts were an adequate basis for personal jurisdiction. Instead, the Court's point was that it was fair for a state court in Pennsylvania to exercise personal jurisdiction over Norfolk Railway based on consent given through its extensive contacts with the state. Justice Gorsuch concluded, "our personal jurisdiction cases have never found a Due Process Clause problem sounding in federalism when an out-of-state defendant submits to suit in the forum State. After all, personal jurisdiction is a personal defense that may be waived or forfeited."[15]

This holding seems clear and straightforward: there can be personal jurisdiction based on consent even if the defendant does not have minimum contacts with the forum state and even if there is neither general nor specific jurisdiction. But the uncertainty comes from Justice Alito's concurring opinion, keeping in mind that he was one of five votes in the majority.

Justice Alito said that if a state can require consent to jurisdiction as a condition for doing business in the state, then there is no problem with personal jurisdiction. But he said that he questions whether states can do this. He suggested that such a requirement violates the dormant commerce clause. He wrote: "I am not convinced, however, that the Constitution permits a State to impose such a submission-to-jurisdiction requirement. A State's assertion of jurisdiction over lawsuits with no real connection to the State may violate fundamental principles that are protected by one or more constitutional provisions or by the very structure of the federal system that the Constitution created. At this point in the development of our constitutional case law, the most appropriate home for these principles is the so-called dormant Commerce Clause."[16]

The dormant commerce clause—which is discussed in Chapter 5—is the principle that state and local governments cannot place a burden on interstate commerce. Justice Alito says that personal jurisdiction is based on "'territorial limitations' on state power."[17] Those territorial limits, in his view, come from the dormant commerce clause. He wrote: "In my view, there is a good prospect that Pennsylvania's assertion of jurisdiction here—over an out-of-state company in a suit brought by an out-of-state plaintiff on claims wholly unrelated to Pennsylvania—violates the Commerce Clause."[18]

He explained that the Pennsylvania law discriminates against out-of-state companies and burdens interstate commerce. He wrote: "There is reason to believe that Pennsylvania's registration-based jurisdiction law discriminates against out-of-state companies. But at the very least, the law imposes a 'significant burden' on interstate commerce by '[r]equiring a foreign corporation . . . to defend itself with reference to all transactions,' including those with no forum connection."[19] He questioned whether Pennsylvania has an interest sufficient to justify such a burden, declaring: "even if some legitimate local interest could be identified, I am skeptical that any local benefits of the State's assertion of jurisdiction in these circumstances could overcome the serious burdens on interstate commerce that it imposes."[20]

There are many ways in which this opinion is remarkable. It is the first time a justice has suggested that the dormant commerce clause, rather than due process, is the basis for personal jurisdiction and limits the ability of a state to exercise jurisdiction over out-of-staters. If so, and if personal jurisdiction is primarily about constitutional limits on a state's territorial reach, then it is unclear why it ever can be gained by consent. Structural constitutional limits cannot be overcome by waiver, which is why subject matter jurisdiction cannot be gained by consent. Personal jurisdiction was thought to be different because it was based on due process and individuals could waive their due process rights. Justice Alito's approach, if followed, would suggest consent is never a sufficient basis for personal jurisdiction.

In terms of the dormant commerce clause, it is unclear why the exercise of personal jurisdiction is a burden on interstate commerce. That is always the threshold question for the dormant commerce clause. Is Justice Alito assuming that some companies will not do business in a state if it means consenting to jurisdiction? And if so, what is the basis for that assumption? Also, it seems unlikely that such state consent laws can be viewed as discriminating against out-of-staters; all companies doing business in the state are required to consent to jurisdiction. And if the law is not discriminatory and a balancing test is used to determine if it violates the dormant commerce clause, why is the state's interest in opening its courts to those injured not sufficient to justify any burden that exists? If ever the Court were to examine the relationship between personal jurisdiction and the dormant commerce clause, it would need to answer these questions.

Justice Alito's opinion thus indicates that the result in this case might be different if it were to ever return to the Supreme Court. Justice Alito would not consider the dormant commerce clause issue at this time because it had not been raised in the lower courts or by the parties. The Supreme Court remanded the case and Norfolk Railway can raise the dormant commerce clause issue in the Pennsylvania courts. Then it can come back to the Court where it would seem that there would be five votes in its favor: Justice Alito on dormant commerce clause grounds and the four dissenting justices to the Court's decision allowing personal jurisdiction.

Justice Barrett wrote for the dissenters. The dissent saw the use of consent as a way to circumvent the limits on personal jurisdiction that the Court had imposed. She wrote: "Such an approach does not formally overrule our traditional contacts-based approach to jurisdiction, but it might as well. By relabeling their long-arm statutes, States may now manufacture 'consent' to personal jurisdiction."[21] She said that allowing personal jurisdiction in this way would "gut" the limits on personal jurisdiction that the Court had created.[22] She would insist that for personal jurisdiction there be either general or specific jurisdiction.

Implications

On the one hand, the Court strongly reaffirmed its precedent from *Pennsylvania Fire* from over a century ago: a state may require that a company register to do business in the state and by registering it consents to personal jurisdiction in the state. The dissent is correct that this provides a way for states, if they choose to adopt such laws, to circumvent limits on personal jurisdiction. We may see more states adopt laws like Pennsylvania's.

On the other hand, there appear to be five votes against this—Justice Alito on dormant commerce clause grounds and the four dissenters based on their view of limits on personal jurisdiction. The Court's holding then seems fragile and may last only until a party can bring a case like this where the dormant commerce clause was raised in the lower courts and by the parties.

Endnotes

1. 143 S. Ct. 2028 (2023).
2. *See Pennoyer v. Neff*, 95 U.S. 714 (1878).
3. *Int'l Shoe Co. v. Wash. Off. of Unemp. Comp. and Placement*, 326 U.S. 310 (1945).
4. 326 U.S. 310 at 320.
5. *Goodyear Dunlop Tires Operations, S. A. v. Brown*, 564 U.S. 915, 924 (2011)
6. *Daimler AG v. Bauman*, 571 U.S. 117, 122 (2014)
7. *Walden v. Fiore*, 571 U.S. 277, 289-290 (2014).
8. *Bristol-Myers Squibb Co. v. Superior Court of Cal,. San Francisco Cty.*, 137 S. Ct. 1773, 1781 (2017).
9. *Id.* at 1780 (quoting *Goodyear Dunlop Tires Operations*, *supra* note 5, at 919).
10. *Carnival Cruise Lines, Inc. v. Shute*, 499 U.S. 585 (1991).
11. 143 S. Ct. 2028 at 2033.
12. 243 U.S. 93 (1917).
13. 143 S. Ct. 2028 at 2033.
14. *Id.* at 2037.
15. *Id.* at 2043.
16. *Id.* at 2047 (Alito, J., dissenting).
17. *Id.* at 2050.
18. *Id.* at 2053.
19. *Id.* at 2053.
20. *Id.* at 2054.
21. *Id.* at 2055 (Barrett, J., dissenting).
22. *Id.* at 2062.

15

Conclusions: Looking Ahead

October Term 2023 will be the third full term with six conservative justices—Roberts, Thomas, Alito, Gorsuch, Kavanaugh, Barrett. In this short time, these six justices have dramatically changed the law, including overruling *Roe v. Wade* and ending affirmative action by colleges and universities. There is every reason to believe that the coming term and the ones to follow will continue to move the law in an overall more conservative direction.

Absent unforeseen circumstances, this likely will continue for many years to come. When the Court begins October Term 2023 on Monday, October 2, Clarence Thomas will be 75 years old, Samuel Alito 73, John Roberts 68, Brett Kavanaugh 58, Neil Gorsuch 56, and Amy Coney Barrett 51. It is easy to imagine these justices being together for another decade or more. Indeed, additional vacancies seem sometime away as Sonia Sotomayor will be 69 when the Court starts the term, Elena Kagan 63, and Ketanji Brown Jackson 53. Indeed, after having had four new justices between 2017 and 2022, we may now have a stretch without changes in the composition of the Court.

The Court usually sets about half of its docket before it adjourns for its summer recess. It is already scheduled to hear a number of potentially very important cases:

Administrative Law

"*Chevron* deference" refers to the principle that federal courts should defer to administrative agencies when they interpret the statutes that they enforce so long as their interpretation is reasonable. It takes its name from the Supreme Court's decision in *Chevron v. Natural Resources Defense Counsel*.[1] There has been speculation for a number of years that the Roberts Court, which has been clear in its desire to rein in the administrative state—such as through the "major questions doctrine," which is discussed in Chapter 7—might overrule, or significantly limit, *Chevron* deference.

Loper Bright Enterprises v. Riamondo poses exactly that issue as the Supreme Court granted review to determine: "Whether the court should overrule *Chevron v. Natural Resources Defense Council*, or at least clarify that statutory silence concerning controversial powers expressly but narrowly granted elsewhere in the statute does not constitute an ambiguity requiring deference to the agency."[2]

The case involves a rule issued by the National Marine Fisheries Service that requires the fishing industry to pay for the costs of observers who monitor compliance with fishery management plans. A group of commercial fishing companies brought a challenge to the rule, but the D.C. Circuit ruled against them, invoking *Chevron* deference.

The petitioner is asking the Court to overrule *Chevron* deference or at least make clear that it does not apply when the terms of a federal statute are clear. The Court will have only eight justices when it hears and decides the case. Justice Jackson is recused, likely because she was on the panel that heard oral arguments in the case in the D.C. Circuit before she was nominated for the Supreme Court.

The context of the case—regulation of commercial fishing—is not likely to attract attention. But for administrative law, this case is a potential blockbuster, raising an issue that many have been expecting the Supreme Court to take.

First Amendment

Several years ago, while President, Donald Trump blocked certain individuals who were critical of his policies from having access to his Twitter feed. The United States Court of Appeals for the Second Circuit ruled that this violated the First Amendment.[3] The Court explained that because Trump used Twitter to conduct government business, he cannot exclude some Americans from reading his posts and responding to them because he does not like their views. The Supreme Court ordered the case dismissed because Trump was no longer President by the time it reached the Court.

The issue is now before the Supreme Court in two less high-profile cases. Interestingly, each of the cases is presented in terms of whether there is state action when public officials block individuals from their personal social media accounts that they use to communicate with the public.

O'Connor-Ratcliff v. Garnier involves two school board members in Southern California who used Twitter and Facebook to communicate with the public.[4] They blocked two parents—Christopher and Kimberly Garnier—who criticized them. The district court and the Ninth Circuit found that the school board members violated the First Amendment because they use Twitter and Facebook to communicate with the public about official government business.

By contrast, in the other case before the Supreme Court, *Lindke v. Freed*, the Sixth Circuit had come to the opposite conclusion.[5] James Freed, the City Manager of Port Huron, Michigan, blocked an individual who criticized him from his Facebook page. The Sixth Circuit said that there was no constitutional violation because Freed did not operate his Facebook page as part of his official duties.

These cases reflect that the Court increasingly must deal with the unique issues that arise because of the internet and social media. As of the end of October Term 2022, the Court had not yet granted review, but it seems very likely they will in two cases involving whether state laws are constitutional when they prevent social media companies from engaging in content moderation. The United States Court of Appeals for the Eleventh Circuit struck down the Florida law,[6] while the Fifth Circuit upheld a similar Texas law.[7] In light of the Circuit split and the importance of the issue, it is easy to predict the Supreme Court will grant certiorari in one or both cases.

Second Amendment

In *New York State Rifle and Pistol Association v. Bruen*, the Supreme Court held that the Second Amendment protects the right of people to have guns in public, and it said that the only type of gun regulations that are allowed are those that were historically permitted.[8] Justice Thomas, writing for the Court in a 6–3 decision, declared: "To justify its regulation, the government may not simply posit that the regulation promotes an important interest. Rather, the government must demonstrate that the regulation is consistent with this Nation's historical tradition of firearm regulation. Only if a firearm regulation is consistent with this Nation's historical tradition may a court conclude that the individual's conduct falls outside the Second Amendment's 'unqualified command.'"[9]

After the Court's decision in *Bruen*, there have been a large number of Second Amendment challenges in lower courts to every type of gun regulation. The first to come to the Supreme Court is *United States v. Rahimi.*[10] A federal statute—18 U.S.C. § 922(g)(8)—prohibits the possession of firearms by persons subject to domestic-violence restraining orders. Zackey Rahimi was under a restraining order for physically assaulting his girlfriend and threatening to kill her. The judge, in imposing the restraining order, barred Rahimi from having a firearm and told him that violating this order would be a federal crime.

When the police searched Rahimi's home pursuant to a warrant, they found a pistol, a rifle, and ammunition—along with a copy of the restraining order. Rahimi was then prosecuted in federal court, convicted, and sentenced to six years in prison. But the United States Court of Appeals for the Fifth Circuit declared unconstitutional the law prohibiting those under restraining orders in domestic violence cases from having firearms. The Court of Appeals focused on the Court's language in *Bruen* and said that this was not a type of regulation that had been historically allowed.

Rahimi will provide an important occasion for the Court to clarify *Bruen*. Few would deny that the government has a great interest in keeping those under restraining orders in domestic violence cases from having guns. Is this interest irrelevant to Second Amendment analysis, as Justice Thomas suggested in *Bruen*? Does it matter that there weren't laws against domestic violence in 1791? Ultimately, the Court will need to clarify how to determine whether gun regulations are constitutional.

Separation of Powers

Rarely does the Supreme Court face the question of whether an entire federal regulatory agency is unconstitutional. But that is the issue in *Consumer Financial Protection Bureau v. Community Financial Services Association of America, Limited.*[11] The Consumer Financial Protection Bureau is an agency created by Congress in 2010 as part of the Dodd-Frank law. The United States Court of Appeals for the Fifth Circuit found that its funding mechanism was unconstitutional and thus effectively declared the agency unconstitutional.

Rather than receiving yearly appropriations from Congress, the CFPB receives funding directly from the Federal Reserve, which collects fees from member banks. The Fifth Circuit said that this violates the constitutional provision that says that "[n]o Money shall be drawn from the Treasury, but in Consequence of Appropriations made by Law."[12] The United States argues that the money for the CFPB has been appropriated by Congress, which directed that the Federal Reserve provide its funds.

The case arose in the context of the CFPB's regulation of the payday lending institution. The Fifth Circuit found the rule invalid on the ground that the CFPB was unconstitutionally funded when the rule was adopted. If the Supreme Court were to affirm, it would then call into question everything that the CFPB ever has done.

Title VII

What injury must a plaintiff in an employment discrimination case demonstrate in order to have a cause of action? That is the issue, in the context of a workplace transfer, in *Muldrow v. City of St. Louis, Missouri.*[13]

Jatonya Muldrow, a sergeant with the St. Louis Police Department, brought a suit claiming employment discrimination based on sex when she was transferred from her position in the Intelligence Division to a patrol position because her supervisor wanted to hire a man for her job. The Eighth Circuit ruled against her, holding that she did not have a claim under Title VII because she had not shown that her transfer resulted in a significant employment disadvantage for her. The Supreme Court granted certiorari on the question: "Whether Title VII of the Civil Rights Act of 1964 prohibits discrimination in transfer decisions absent a separate court determination that the transfer decision caused a signification disadvantage."[14]

Conclusion

These, of course, are just a few of the cases to be decided in October Term 2023. There is no doubt that it will be another momentous year in the United States Supreme Court.

Endnotes

1. 467 U.S. 837 (1984).
2. *Loper Bright Enters. v. Raimondo*, 45 F.4th 359 (D.C. Cir. 2022).
3. *Knight First Amend. Inst. of Columbia Univ. v. Trump*, 928 F.3d 226 (2d Cir. 2019).
4. *Garnier v. O'Connor-Ratcliff*, 41 F.4th 1158 (7th Cir. 2022).
5. *Lindke v. Freed*, 37 F.4th 1199 (6th Cir. 2022).
6. *NetChoice v. Atty. Gen., Fla.*, 34 F.4th 1196 (11th Cir. 2022).
7. *NetChoice, L.L.C. v. Paxton*, 49 F.4th 439 (5th Cir. 2022).
8. *N.Y. State Rifle & Pistol Ass'n v. Bruen*, 142 S. Ct. 2111 (2022).
9. *Id.* at 2126.
10. *United States v. Rahimi*, 61 F.4th 443 (5th Cir. 2023).
11. *Cmty. Fin. Servs. Ass'n of Am. v. Consumer Fin. Prot. Bureau*, 51 F.4th 616 (5th Cir. 2022).
12. U.S. Const. art. I § 9, cl. 7.
13. *Muldrow v. City of St. Louis*, 30 F.4th 680 (8th Cir. 2022).
14. *Muldrow v. City of St. Louis, Missouri*, SCOTUSblog, https://www.scotusblog.com/case-files/cases/muldrow-v-city-of-st-louis-missouri/.

Index

A

Abitron Austria GmbH v. Hetronic International, Inc., 116–117
administrative law, 134
Administrative Procedure Act, 64
adoption and foster care, 101–105
affirmative action, 13–22
  Jackson on, 6–7
  precedent, 13–15
  in *Students for Fair Admission* cases, 5, 15–22
aiding-and-abetting liability, 84–85, 86
Alabama redistricting case. *See Allen v. Milligan*
Alassaf, Nawras, 84
Alito, Samuel
  in *Abitron Austria GmbH v. Hetronic International, Inc.*, 117
  in *Allen v. Milligan*, 56
  in *Glacier Northwest, Inc. v. International Brotherhood of Teamsters Local No. 174*, 122
  in *Groff v. DeJoy*, 28–29
  in *Mallory v. Norfolk Southern Railway Co.*, 128–130
  in *Marion County v. Talevski*, 27
  in *Reed v. Goertz*, 38
  in *Sackett v. Environmental Protection Agency*, 63, 65
  in *Santos-Zacaria v. Garland*, 96
  in *United States v. Texas*, 72
Allen v. Milligan, 6, 54–56
American Farm Bureau Federation, 46
Andy Warhol Foundation for the Visual Arts v. Goldsmith, 109–113
antidiscrimination laws, state, 4–5, 77–80
Antiterrorism and Effective Death Penalty Act (AEDPA), 32–33
Arizona Supreme Court, 39, 40
Arizona v. Navajo Nation, 105–107
Attorney General, Florida v. Netchoice, LLC, 86

B

Bakke decision, 13–14
balancing test and the dormant commerce clause, 48–49, 50
Barrett, Amy Coney
  in *Biden v. Nebraska*, 75
  in *Counterman v. Colorado*, 83
  in *Cruz v. Arizona*, 40
  in *Glacier Northwest, Inc. v. International Brotherhood of Teamsters Local No. 174*, 120, 121
  in *Haaland v. Brackeen*, 102–104
  in *Mallory v. Norfolk Southern Railway Co.*, 130
  in *National Pork Producers v. Ross*, 49
  in *United States v. Hansen*, 90
  in *United States v. Texas*, 71
Biden, Joe. *See Biden v. Nebraska*
Biden v. Nebraska, 3–4, 8, 69, 73–76
Board of Immigration Appeals (BIA), 95, 96
Brackeen, Chad and Jennifer, 102
Bristol-Myers Squibb Co. v. Superior Court of Cal., San Francisco Cty., 126

Brnovich v. Democratic National Committee, 53, 54
Bruton v. United States, 35, 36
Bush v. Gore, 57
businesses
and the dormant commerce clause, 45–51
and economic consequences of strikes, 119–123
and personal jurisdiction, 125–131
rights of, to discriminate, 4–5, 77–80

C
California voter initiatives. *See* Proposition 12; Proposition 209
case numbers, 2–3
Chevron v. Natural Resources Defense Council, 134
civil rights, 25–30
Groff v. DeJoy, 4, 27–30
Health and Hospital Corporation of Marion County v. Talevski, 25–27
Muldrow v. City of St. Louis, Missouri, 137–138
See also Voting Rights Act
Clean Water Act, 63–67
codefendants and the Confrontation Clause, 34–36
college and university admissions. *See* affirmative action
Colorado Supreme Court, 81, 82
Commerce Clause, 66. *See also* dormant commerce clause
commercial fishing regulation, 134
compelling interest
and affirmative action, 14, 15, 17, 19
and sexual orientation discrimination, 78, 79–80
Condé Nast, 110, 112
confessions and codefendants, 34–36
Confrontation Clause, 34–36
Congress, Court's lack of deference to, 4
conscientious objection to providing services, 78, 80
consent, as basis for personal jurisdiction, 126–130
Consumer Financial Protection Bureau v. Community Financial Services Association of America, Limited, 137
copyright law, fair use in, 109–113
Cordero-Garcia, Fernando, 91–92
Counterman, Billy Raymond, 81–82
Counterman v. Colorado, 77, 80–83
criminal law and procedure, 31–40
Confrontation Clause, 34–36
habeas corpus, 7–8, 32–34
statute of limitations and DNA evidence, 37–38
Supreme Court review of state court decisions, 39–40
Cruz, John Montenegro, 39, 40
Cruz v. Arizona, 39–40

D
Department of Education v. Brown, 73
Department of Homeland Security, 70, 72, 91
dilution, trademark, 114, 115
discrimination
and rights of businesses, 4–5, 77–80
and Title VII, 137–138
diversity in college admissions. *See* affirmative action
DNA evidence, 37–38
domestic violence restraining orders and gun possession, 136–137
dormant commerce clause, 45–51, 128–131
due process
and personal jurisdiction, 125, 127, 128–129
procedural due process claims, 37, 38
and vagueness, 65

E
Eighth Circuit Court of Appeals, 32, 138
election law, 52–60
  Allen v. Milligan, 6, 54–56
  Moore v. Harper, 56–60
Elections Clause, 59
Eleventh Circuit Court of Appeals, 37, 135
environmental law, 63–67
Environmental Protection Agency, 64–67
equal protection
  and affirmative action, 16, 17, 19
  and election redistricting, 55
  and the Indian Child Welfare Act, 104–105
  Jackson on, 7
ethical issues, 2
executive power, 69–76
  Biden v. Nebraska, 73–76
  United States v. Texas, 70–73
exhaustion of remedies in removal proceedings, 95–96
expression, freedom of. *See* freedom of speech
extraterritorial application of the Lanham Act, 116–117

F
fair use in copyright law, 109–113
Federal Nursing Home Reform Act, 26, 27
Fifth Circuit Court of Appeals, 37, 70, 95–96, 102, 135, 136, 137
First Amendment, 135. *See also* freedom of speech
First Circuit Court of Appeals, 16
Fisher v. University of Texas at Austin, 15–16
foster care and adoption, 101–105
Fourteenth Amendment, 17, 127
Fourth Circuit Court of Appeals, 92
Frankfurter, Felix, 46
Freed, James, 135
freedom of speech
  Counterman v. Colorado, 77–86
  Gonzalez v. Google, 85–86
  303 Creative LLC v. Elenis, 77–80
  Twitter v. Taamneh, 83–85, 86
  United States v. Hansen, 89–91

G
Garnier, Christopher and Kimberly, 135
gerrymandering. *See* election law
Glacier Northwest, Inc. v. International Brotherhood of Teamsters Local No. 174, 119–123
Goldsmith, Lynn, 109–110, 112
Gonzalez, Nohemi, 85
Gonzalez v. Google, 83, 85–86
Gorsuch, Neil
  in *Arizona v. Navajo Nation,* 107
  in *Haaland v. Brackeen,* 101, 105
  in *Jack Daniel's Properties, Inc. v. VIP Products LLC,* 115–116
  in *Mallory v. Norfolk Southern Railway Co.,* 127–128
  in *Marion County v. Talevski,* 27
  in *National Pork Producers v. Ross,* 47–48
  in *Students for Fair Admission v. Harvard College,* 18
  in *303 Creative LLC v. Elenis,* 78–79
  in *United States v. Texas,* 71
Groff, Gerald, 28, 29
Groff v. DeJoy, 4, 27–30
Grutter v. Bollinger, 14, 17–18
gun regulations, 136–137

H
Haaland v. Brackeen, 101–105
habeas corpus, 7–8, 32–34
Hansen, Helman, 89–90
Harvard College. *See Students for Fair Admission v. Harvard College*
Hetronic International, Inc. *See Abitron Austria GmbH v. Hetronic International, Inc.*

Higher Education Relief Opportunities for Students Act (HEROES Act), 73–76
history, views on the lessons of, 19–20
Hunter, Joseph, 34, 35

I
Immigration and National Act, 92, 94, 95
immigration law, 89–96
 Pugin v. Garland, 91–95
 Santos-Zacaria v. Garland, 95–96
 United States v. Hansen, 89–91
 United States v. Texas, 69, 70–73
independent state legislature theory, 2, 5–6, 57–60
Indian Child Welfare Act, 101–105
Indian law, 101–107
 Arizona v. Navajo Nation, 105–107
 Haaland v. Brackeen, 101–105
infringement
 of copyright, 109–113
 of trademark, 114–115
intellectual property, 109–117
 Abitron Austria GmbH v. Hetronic International, Inc., 116–117
 Andy Warhol Foundation for the Visual Arts v. Goldsmith, 109–113
 Jack Daniel's Properties, Inc. v. VIP Products LLC, 113–116
International Brotherhood of Teamsters Local No. 174. *See Glacier Northwest, Inc. v. International Brotherhood of Teamsters Local No. 174*
International Shoe v. State of Washington, 125, 126
international terrorism, 84–85
internet and social media, 83–86, 135
interstate commerce. *See* Commerce Clause; dormant commerce clause
Islamic State of Iraq and Syria (ISIS), 84

J
Jack Daniel's Properties, Inc. v. VIP Products LLC, 113–116
Jackson, Ketanji Brown
 first year on court of, 6–8
 in *Glacier Northwest, Inc. v. International Brotherhood of Teamsters Local No. 174,* 122
 in *Jones v. Hendrix,* 34
 in *Marion County v. Talevski,* 26–27
 in *Samia v. United States,* 36
 in *Santos-Zacaria v. Garland,* 96
 in *Students for Fair Admission v. Harvard College,* 18–19
 in *United States v. Hansen,* 90–91
Jones, Marcus DeAngelo, 32–33
Jones v. Hendrix, 7–8, 32–34
judicial review
 federal review of state law, 5–6, 31, 37–38, 39–40
 by state courts, 58–59
jurisdiction, personal. *See* personal jurisdiction
justices, age of, 133

K
Kagan, Elena
 in *Andy Warhol Foundation for the Visual Arts v. Goldsmith,* 112
 in *Biden v. Nebraska,* 74, 75
 in *Counterman v. Colorado,* 82
 in *Jack Daniel's Properties, Inc. v. VIP Products LLC,* 113–115
 in *Sackett v. Environmental Protection Agency,* 66–67
 in *Samia v. United States,* 36
Kavanaugh, Brett
 in *Allen v. Milligan,* 55–56
 in *Arizona v. Navajo Nation,* 106–107
 in *Haaland v. Brackeen,* 104
 in *National Pork Producers v. Ross,* 50

- percentage of time in the majority, 3
- in *Pugin v. Garland,* 92–93
- in *Reed v. Goertz,* 37, 38
- in *Sackett v. Environmental Protection Agency,* 67
- on statutory precedent, 4
- in *Students for Fair Admission v. Harvard College,* 18
- in *United States v. Texas,* 70–71, 72

Kennedy, Anthony, 15

L

labor law, 119–123
Lanham Act, 114, 115, 116–117
Lee, Catherine, 34
LGBTQ rights. *See* sexual orientation discrimination
liability for aiding-and-abetting, 84–85, 86
Linda R.S. v. Richard D., 70–71
Lindke v. Freed, 135
Loper Bright Enterprises v. Riamondo, 134
Lynch v. Arizona, 39, 40

M

Maine v. Thiboutot, 26
major questions doctrine, 70, 74–75, 76
Mallory, Robert, 127
Mallory v. Norfolk Southern Railway Co., 125, 126–131
Marbury v. Madison, 58–59
Masharipov, Abdulkadir, 84, 85
Missouri Higher Education Loan Authority (MOHELA), 73–74
Moore v. Harper, 5–6, 56–60
Muldrow, Jatonya, 137–138
Muldrow v. City of St. Louis, Missouri, 137–138

N

Nailati, Mana, 89
National Labor Relations Act (NLRA), 119–123
National Labor Relations Board, 120–121, 123
National Marine Fisheries Service, 134
National Pork Producers v. Ross, 45–51
Native Americans. *See* Indian law
NetChoice, LLC v. Paxton, 86
New York State Rifle and Pistol Association v. Bruen, 136–137
New York Times v. Sullivan, 82, 83
Ninth Circuit Court of Appeals, 49–50, 91–92, 106, 135
Norfolk Southern Railway. *See Mallory v. Norfolk Southern Railway Co.*
North Carolina redistricting case. *See Moore v. Harper*
North Carolina Supreme Court, 57, 58

O

obstruction of justice, 91–95
O'Connor, Sandra Day, 14, 18
O'Connor-Ratcliff v. Garnier, 135
October Term 2004, 3
October Term 2021, 1
October Term 2022, 1–6, 8, 9. *See also* specific cases
October Term 2023, 134–138
oral arguments, length of, 3
"Orange Prince" photo case. *See Andy Warhol Foundation for the Visual Arts v. Goldsmith*
overbreadth standard, 90–91

P

parody and trademark law, 113–116
Pennsylvania Fire Ins. Co. of Philadelphia v. Gold Issue Mining & Milling Co., 127–128
personal jurisdiction, 125–131
Pike v. Bruce Church, Inc., 48, 49, 50
postconviction DNA testing law, 37–38
Powell, Lewis, 14
precedent
- in affirmative action cases, 13–15
- overruling of, 5
- statutory *vs.* constitutional, 4, 55–56
- *See also* specific cases

President of the United States, Court's lack of deference to, 3–4
presidential powers. *See* executive power
procedural due process claims, 37, 38
Proposition 12 (California), 46–47
Proposition 209 (California), 20–21
public accommodation laws, 79–80. *See also* reasonable accommodation
public approval/disapproval of the Supreme Court, 2
Pugin, Jean Francois, 91, 92
Pugin v. Garland, 91–95

R

racial discrimination. *See* civil rights; Voting Rights Act
racial preferences
  and the Indian Child Welfare Act, 104–105
  Jackson on, 6–7
  See also affirmative action
Rahimi, Zackey, 136
Rapanos v. United States, 64, 65
reasonable accommodation, 27–30
recklessness and true threats, 81, 82–83
redistricting, election. *See* election law
Reed, Rodney, 37–38
Reed v. Goertz, 37–38
Regents of the University of California v. Bakke, 13–14
Rehaif v. United States, 32–33
Rehnquist, William, 57
Reina nightclub attack, 84–85
religious protections, 4, 27–30. *See also* conscientious objection to providing services
restraining orders and gun possession, 136–137
rhetoric in opinions, 8
Roberts, John
  in *Allen v. Milligan,* 54–55, 56
  in *Biden v. Nebraska,* 69, 73–75
  on Court rhetoric, 8
  as majority opinion writer, 2
  in *Moore v. Harper,* 5–6, 58–60
  in *National Pork Producers v. Ross,* 49–50
  percentage of time in the majority, 3
  in *Students for Fair Admission v. Harvard College,* 13, 16–17, 21
Rogers v. Grimaldi, 114–115, 116
Rooker-Feldman doctrine, 38
Rucho v. Common Cause, 53

S

Sackett, Michael and Chantell, 64
Sackett v. Environmental Protection Agency, 63–67
same-sex weddings. *See* sexual orientation discrimination
Samia, Adam, 34, 35
Samia v. United States, 34–36
San Diego Building Trades Council v. Garmon, 120, 121–122
Santos-Zacaria, Estrella, 95–96
Santos-Zacaria v. Garland, 95–96
saving clause, 32, 33
scrutiny in racial classification, 13–14
Second Amendment, 136–137
Second Circuit Court of Appeals, 114, 135
separation of powers, 137
sex discrimination, 137–138
sexual orientation discrimination, 78, 79
Shelby County v. Holder, 53
Simmons v. South, 39, 40
Sixth Amendment, 35, 36
Sixth Circuit Court of Appeals, 135
Smith, Lorie, 77–78, 79
social media and the internet, 83–86, 135
Sotomayor, Sonia
  in *Andy Warhol Foundation for the Visual Arts v. Goldsmith,* 111–112
  in *Counterman v. Colorado,* 82–83

in *Cruz v. Arizona,* 39–40
in *Groff v. DeJoy,* 29
in *Jack Daniel's Properties, Inc. v. VIP Products LLC,* 115
in *Jones v. Hendrix,* 33–34
in *National Pork Producers v. Ross,* 48–49
in *Pugin v. Garland,* 93–95
in *Students for Fair Admissions v. Harvard College,* 18
in *303 Creative LLC v. Elenis,* 5, 79–80
speech, freedom of. *See* freedom of speech
spending clause laws, 26–27
St. Louis Police Department, 137–138
standing, question of
in *Biden v. Nebraska,* 69, 73–76
in *United States v. Texas,* 69, 70–71
stare decisis. See precedent; specific cases
state antidiscrimination laws, 4–5, 77–80
state challenges to executive power, 69–76
Biden v. Nebraska, 73–76
United States v. Texas, 70–73
state court decisions, federal review of, 5–6, 31, 37–38, 39–40
state governments, Court's lack of deference to, 4–5
statute of limitations and DNA evidence, 37–38
statutory *vs.* constitutional precedent, 4, 55–56
Stewart, Potter, 48
Stillwell, Carl, 34–35, 36
student loan forgiveness program, 3–4, 69, 73–76
Students for Fair Admission v. Harvard College, 5, 7, 13, 15–22
Students for Fair Admission v. University of North Carolina, 15–22

T

Tenth Amendment, 103–104
Tenth Circuit Court of Appeals, 78, 116–117
terrorist activity, aiding-and-abetting, 84–85
Texas Court of Criminal Appeals, 37, 38
Thomas, Clarence
in *Allen v. Milligan,* 56
in Confrontation Clause, 35, 36
in *Counterman v. Colorado,* 83
in *Glacier Northwest, Inc. v. International Brotherhood of Teamsters Local No. 174,* 121–122
Jackson's disagreement with, 7
in *Jones v. Hendrix,* 33
in *Marion County v. Talevski,* 27
in *Moore v. Harper,* 58, 60
in *New York State Rifle and Pistol Association v. Bruen,* 136
in *Sackett v. Environmental Protection Agency,* 66
in *Samia v. United States,* 35–36
in *Students for Fair Admission v. Harvard College,* 17–18
in *Twitter v. Tamneh,* 84–85
Thornburgh v. Gingles, 54–56
303 Creative LLC v. Elenis, 4–5, 77–80
Title VI of the Civil Rights Act of 1964, 14, 16, 18
Title VII of the Civil Rights Act of 1964, 4, 27–30, 137–138
trademark law, 113–117
Trans World Airlines, Inc. v. Hardison, 28
transformative *vs.* derivative use in copyright law, 110–113
Treaty of 1868, 105–107
true threats and freedom of speech, 80–83
Trump, Donald, 1, 58, 73, 135
Twitter v. Taamneh, 77, 83–86

U

unanimous decisions, 3
undue hardship and reasonable accommodation, 27–30
union liability for economic consequences of strikes, 119–123
United States District Court for the Western District of Missouri, 32
United States v. Hansen, 89–91
United States v. Rahimi, 136–137
United States v. Stevens, 90–91
United States v. Texas, 70–73, 89
United States v. Watts, 80–81
University of Michigan Law School, 14
University of North Carolina. *See Students for Fair Admission v. University of North Carolina*

V

vagueness, 65
Vanity Fair, 110
VIP Products LLC, 113–115
Voting Rights Act, 6, 53, 54–56, 60
voting rights cases. *See* election law

W

Walden v. Fiore, 126
Warhol, Andy, 110
water rights, 105–107
Watts, Robert, 80–81
West Virginia v. EPA, 75
wetlands protection. *See* environmental law
Winters doctrine, 105–106